Audiobook
ACTING

Audiobook
ACTING

A MASTERCLASS
IN THE ART
AND THE BUSINESS

Taro Meyer

SILMAN-JAMES PRESS   LOS ANGELES

10 9 8 7 6 5 4 3 2 1

Library of Congress Cataloging-in-Publication Data

Names: Meyer, Taro, author.
Title: Audiobook acting : a masterclass in the art and the business
/ by Taro Meyer.
Description: Los Angeles : Silman-James Press, [2022]
Identifiers: LCCN 2022058078 (print) |
LCCN 2022058079 (ebook)
ISBN 9781935247302 (paperback) |
ISBN 9781935247913 (ebook)
Subjects: LCSH: Voice culture. | Oral reading. | Audiobooks. |
Sound recordings--Production and direction. |
Voice actors and actresses--Vocational guidance.
Classification: LCC PN4197 .M49 2022 (print) |
LCC PN4197 (ebook) |
DDC
808.5/4--dc23/eng/20230206
LC record available at https://lccn.loc.gov/2022058078
LC ebook record available at https://lccn.loc.gov/2022058079

Cover design by Wade Lageose for Lageose Design

Printed and bound in the United States of America

SILMAN-JAMES PRESS
www.silmanjamespress.com

Contents

List of Workouts

Acknowledgments

Tremendous thanks to this book's editor, Eleanore Speert, whose brilliance and wonderful sense of humor make working with her an absolute joy. I am deeply grateful for the insights of my early readers: Neil Mitchell, Kevin Isola, Pete Pantelis. Much appreciation for the wonderful, creative people I've worked with in the audiobook industry through the years. And a special note of thanks to Gwen Feldman of Silman-James Press, for her belief in this book.

Introduction

'In the beginning was the word.'
Then came the story.

I was sitting with the late, brilliant actress, Oscar nominee Ruby Dee (*American Gangster, Do the Right Thing, Raisin in the Sun*), in The Dorothy Chandler Pavilion in Los Angeles, scene of the 49th annual Grammy Awards. The audiobook I had produced and directed, Ruby and her late husband Ossie Davis's autobiography, *With Ossie and Ruby: In This Life Together*, had been nominated for a Grammy. As we watched other awards being given out, I suddenly noticed that Ruby was quietly mouthing something. "Are you okay?" I whispered.

"Oh yes," she smiled. "I'm just rehearsing what I'm going to say when we win."

Although she was teasing about her surety of winning, *With Ossie and Ruby: In This Life Together* did win a Grammy and as Ruby and I excitedly stood onstage, she looked out over the audience and began to speak. "In the beginning," she said, "was the word. And then came the story."

Story is at the very heart of the human experience. It is embedded in our creative DNA. Of all the methods we've used to communicate stories, our voice has a power like no other. The old the tribal storytellers told their tales before evening fires to the small group gathered before them in the dark. But today, thanks to technology, you, the modern storyteller—the Audiobook Actor—can sit in a studio before a microphone and reach thousands of listeners.

Ruby Dee's power as an Audiobook Actor rested not only on her understanding of the primality, the vital power of story, but because she came to each one from the center of her being, creating a one-of-a-kind performance.

As a longtime audiobook producer and director, I've had the joy of guiding many Audiobook Actors, both newcomers and pros, into creating rich, expressive and unique performances. With more and more actors entering the field, and increasingly working in home studios without the benefit of a director, I wanted to make the techniques I've successfully used in the studio available in one resource.

Audiobook Acting gives you those techniques, enabling you to release the power of your imagination and master the skill set needed to make each story you read a creative and engaging experience for both you and the listener. This book is structured to feel as close to personal coaching sessions as possible, providing a comprehensive, step-by-step approach that will allow you to explore, practice and proceed at your own pace.

Whether you are a professional actor or a newcomer you'll learn how to bring your individual talents and interpretive insights to the fore within the unique demands of the art of Audiobook Acting. It's an art in which, rather than develop a single role, you will give voice to multiple characters and navigate the shifting landscape of an entire book.

As you move through this book's chapters, you'll learn how to blend your creative interpretation with the author's vision. You'll acquire the ability to give multiple characters identifiable voices and personalities and deliver believable dialogue between characters who you alone are voicing.

- ◆ If you're a professional actor, you'll acquire new skills and learn to integrate your stage and screen techniques with the distinctive techniques of audiobook work. While you're trained to use your entire physicality for film and theater performances, for audiobook work you must convey everything through your voice. That brilliant facial expression or fabulous physical movement you came up with to reveal a world of meaning on stage or film? It doesn't work for audiobooks. It's all in the voice.

◆ Acting students will be able build audiobook acting skills from the ground up. You'll learn the proper breathing technique that gives you a sustained vocal performance. You'll master the critical approaches to audiobook acting and emerge armed with the know-how to audition successfully for audiobook jobs. This can be a tremendous plus, as actors find that they can often carve a niche in the audiobook world while working in other media.

◆ Actors focusing on voice-over work – telling short, compact stories for commercials or narrated videos – you will learn how to switch over and create long-form storytelling.

◆ Authors can learn to use these techniques to improve their readings. I've worked with many authors who are surprised when they discover that just speaking the words they wrote does not convey the intent they had when writing the book. They often want to "try that again." And some get winded during the session. Learning proper breathing technique, as well as the acting techniques in this book, won't turn you into an actor, but you won't have to "try that again," too many times.

◆ Professionals from other fields are interested in learning *Audiobook Acting* techniques. A minister recently began studying to improve the delivery of his sermons. I worked with one gentleman who coached not-for-profit Boards of Directors and wanted to apply these skills in his presentations. Story is so often used to frame a business's focus, develop teamwork or encourage investment, that the ability to tell your story powerfully is an important business asset.

◆ Teachers can use these techniques as a part of reading instruction for young children. Helping children assess and convey a character's point of view or express how different characters feel, can become an important adjunct to teaching reading skills and can help your students develop a greater ability for story analysis.

As you work, take your time and do the workouts (exercises) that have been provided. As you become familiar with the audiobook acting techniques presented here, implementing them will become easier and easier. You will cultivate an arsenal of skills you'll be able to apply to any book both creatively and efficiently.

PART ONE

YOUR VOICE

The power of the human voice is infinite. It can inspire us, bring us to tears, foster hope, evoke panic or cause laughter. And you don't need a beautiful sounding voice to do all that. In fact, for audiobook acting there is no right or wrong voice: deep or sonorous, rough or silky, high or quirky, it doesn't matter. What does matter is being able to:

♦ Unlock the power of your unique vocal identity.

♦ Use the full range of your voice without strain.

♦ Use your voice to convey emotion, ideas and imagery.

♦ Read for extended periods of time without tiring.

The ability to achieve this rests on the foundations of proper breathing and vocal freedom.

1

Diaphragmatic Breathing

And when I breathed, my breath was lightning.
—Black Elk[1]

B reath is the starting point for your vocal sound. And while that sound is physical—the result of air passing between your vocal cords, the size and shape of those cords and your resonating chambers—breath is the lightening, the power source for that sound.

While breathing is mostly an involuntary action, it is partly under our conscious control. For the audiobook actor, this conscious control is vital. Diaphragmatic breathing is how you can maximize this control.

Here's how it works:

The diaphragm is a dome shaped muscle attached to the base of your lungs, separating your chest from your abdomen. Whenever you breathe your diaphragm goes into action. As you inhale, it contracts and moves downward, and your ribcage expands. This action allows your lungs to expand. When you exhale, the diaphragm relaxes, and your lungs expel the air.

As adults, many of us have learned to do shallow, chest breathing. This means that the diaphragm doesn't fully contract, causing our

---

[1] John G. Neihardt, *Black Elk Speaks.*

intercostal muscles as well as the muscles in our neck to take up the slack. We take a breath, raising our chest and shoulders. Not only is there less air taken in that way, but that action constricts our throat and puts pressure on our vocal cords.

Diaphragmatic breathing is deep breathing. By contracting the diaphragm more fully, your lungs will open more fully, allowing you to take in more air. When you exhale, you're gently contracting your abdominals, controlling the flow of air as it leaves your lungs. This is actually the natural way to breathe. Look at a baby breathing; her tummy expands and contracts.

Diaphragmatic breathing is key to giving your voice freedom and flexibility because it does not put pressure on your throat and vocal cords.

Diaphragmatic breathing is a mind/body link that's good for overall well-being. It stimulates the parasympathetic nervous system resulting in relaxation and slowing of the heart rate, which leads to a greater sense of well-being and focus. It is energizing, a big plus for an audiobook actor working in a studio for several hours. Following are a few diaphragmatic breathing workouts that will start you on the path to proper, free, healthy breathing.

Diaphragmatic Breathing Workouts

Do these every day, several times a day, and breathing diaphragmatically will quickly become natural again. Begin by doing them at home in a comfortable setting, because you may feel a little light-headed at first. Start with a few repetitions of each workout and build up slowly.

In daily life we usually breathe through our nose, but in some of these exercises you'll be breathing through your mouth. That's how you'll be breathing as you narrate a book, so being comfortable breathing that way will make it second nature for you in the studio.

These workouts are to be done gently, without pushing or straining. Never do anything to the point of discomfort. If you do feel pain or discomfort when doing any of the workouts, check with to your doctor before continuing them.

Finding the Feeling

1. Lie down.

2. Pant. Breathe in and out rapidly through your mouth. Your belly should start to move up and down quickly. Your shoulders should stay down and relaxed. If you lightly touch your lower ribs, you'll feel them expand and contract a bit too, as will your back. This will happen naturally, so you don't have to think about it. Focus your attention on your belly. To make the correct movements even more visible, put a lightweight book or magazine on your stomach. You'll see the book or magazine moving up and down.

3. Slow your panting down so that you're breathing at a normal rate but still breathing the same way, diaphragmatically and gently.

4. Note that your abdominal muscles contract as you exhale. Your pelvic muscles will contract as well; you aren't just sucking your stomach in, you're contracting the muscles. This action supports your breath and will help you moderate the amount of breath you exhale, and it will help you control the speed of your exhalation.

Once you are able to recognize the difference between chest and diaphragmatic breathing, move on to the following workouts.

Read the directions for each workout completely before you begin. The more you practice, the more you'll be able to extend the counts for each workout. That will come naturally as you become more comfortable with this way of breathing.

Inhale / Hold / Exhale / Hold (Mouth Breathing)

Do this workout in front of a mirror at first so that you can check your posture and make sure your shoulders aren't moving up and down as you breathe.

1. Stand or sit up straight and comfortably, feet about hips-width apart.

2. Inhale slowly through your mouth, to a count of two.

   Your mouth and lips should be relaxed.

   Maintain your upright, relaxed posture. There should be no tension in your neck and shoulders.

   Your abdomen will expand as your diaphragm contracts and pulls downward.

   It will feel as if your breath is moving into the lower part of your abdomen first and then filling your chest. (Of course, your breath is only going into your lungs.)

   Your ribcage will expand.

3. Close your mouth and hold your breath for the count of two.

4. Exhale through your mouth to a count of four (twice the count of the inhalation).

   You'll be contracting your abdominal muscles first and then your intercostal muscles (in the rib cage) as you exhale, until you've expelled all the air.

5. Once the air is expelled, close your mouth and hold your breath for a count of two.

   There will be little air in your lungs. Your abdominal muscles will be contracted, holding the 'empty' position. Don't try to empty your lungs to a point that is uncomfortable or where you feel as if you desperately need to take a breath. If you can't hold for a count of two, breathe sooner. You'll become more proficient as you practice. Here's the count sequence in simple form:

Inhale: 2, Hold: 2, Exhale: 4, Hold: 2.

6. Repeat the workout a few times but only for as long as you're using diaphragmatic breathing and are comfortable. Again, this might make you feel a little lightheaded at first, so be sure to begin practicing at home and never do anything to the point of discomfort.

7. Once you're managing this flow of air comfortably, increase the count: Inhale: 3, Hold: 3, Exhale: 6, Hold: 3.

8. Continue increasing the count as long as you are comfortable and not straining.

Be aware of how your abdominal muscles contribute to controlling the flow of air. Eventually, using your abdominal muscles this way will become natural, but for now take note of the process.

Repeat the workout using the new, higher count several times until you're comfortable, then increase your count again, always making the exhalation twice as long as the inhalation and the hold.

Nostril Alternation

1. Sit comfortably with erect posture.

   Your mouth is closed.

   Place your right forefinger on the right side of your nose, gently closing it so that you can only breathe through your left nostril.

2. Inhale slowly through your left nostril to a count of two.

3. Place your middle finger on your left nostril.

   Hold both nostrils closed for the count of two.

   Keep your chest and shoulders relaxed.

4. Remove your forefinger from your right nostril and slowly exhale to a count of four as you gently contract your stomach muscles. The feeling is that you are gently pressing those muscles in as you contract. Feel the sense of support this provides.

5. Hold your two fingers on both nostrils, closing them both for a count of two, while keeping your abdominal muscles contracted.

6. Keeping your middle finger on your left nostril, release your forefinger from the right nostril and inhale for a count of two.

   Here's the count sequence in simple form:

   Close right nostril, inhale into left nostril for a count of 2.

   Close both nostrils and hold for a count of 2.

   Release right nostril and exhale for a count of 4.

   Close both nostrils for a count of 2.

   Close left nostril, release right nostril, inhale for a count of 2.

   If exhaling for a count of 4 is stressful, reduce the count to 1-1-2-1.

7. Repeat the workout. When the count becomes easy to manage, increase it, always exhaling for twice as long as you inhale. Your goal is to increase the count, thus improving your breath control.

Do these workouts several times a day and soon diaphragmatic breathing will become the way you breathe all the time. Diaphragmatic breathing not only increases your breath capacity, but it is the foundation for a free and flexible sound.

2

Vocal Placement

Now where'd I put that?

—Everybody at some point

In all mediums of acting, you'll hear people, including me, talk about proper placement in regard to strengthening and using your voice. That makes it seem like you can actually place your voice somewhere, e.g., place it in *the mask*,[1] place it *off the throat*,[2] or place it *forward*.[3]

But you can't really place your voice anywhere.

Proper placement is actually the state in which the muscles involved in speech (or singing) are aligned properly, and the sound you are making is free and doesn't hurt your throat. The result is that your voice will sound and feel like it's placed forward, as opposed to jammed up in the back of your throat or coming straight out of your nose.

Of course, you can't consciously control every muscle involved in proper alignment. Imagine trying to walk across a room by consciously

---

[1] *The mask* refers to the frontal cavities of the face and the upper front palate.

[2] *Off the throat* means taking the pressure off your throat and using diaphragmatic breathing.

[3] *Placing it forward* means your voice sounds like it's coming from the front of your face, not from back in your throat or through your nose.

determining the action and position of every single nerve signal and muscle involved in walking.

You wouldn't move an inch.

Instead, when we want to walk, having learned what walking is, our autonomous system takes over and off we go.

Proper vocal alignment works the same way, and it begins with a diaphragmatic breath.

You breathe in, then, when you exhale, you contract your abdominals just as you did in the breathing workouts, but now you add sound to the breath.

As you use your diaphragmatic breathing, you'll recognize and feel the free sound in your throat and body. You won't be raising your chest and shoulders or squeezing your throat. It will feel as if there's a column of air from your abdominals to your lips, and your voice is floating on that column. This is called 'speaking on the breath.' As you begin to speak with that free sound, just as with walking, your brain will recognize how to position your vocal apparatus to get that free forward sound, and off you go. This type of practice helps you access the full range of your voice – your highs and lows—and can help expand it.

Speaking on the Breath Workouts

Start slowly and build up the length of time you do each workout. Soon, speaking on the breath will become natural. And these are perfect warm-ups to use before any recording session.

As you are practicing, if you feel your voice getting stuck in your throat rather than feeling free, turn your head slowly from side to side as you do the workout. Do this very gently and with no tension—as if your neck and head are floating on the top of your torso. Do not turn your head that way if it makes you dizzy or uncomfortable.

Huuuummmm on the Floor

1. Lie down on your back.

2. Inhale deeply and then release the breath.

   Just like in the breathing exercises, your diaphragm is the driving force behind the breath.

3. Take a few breaths and when you're sure you're breathing diaphragmatically, breath in, then exhale on the sound: Huuuummmm.

   Say Huuuummmm during the entire exhalation.

   Notice how the sound vibration feels as if it's coming from the front of your face. The ending mmmm sound helps you to feel that very easily.

4. Repeat the above, but now extend the time you say Huuuummmm.

5. Next, try saying: Huuuummmmuuuummmmuuuummmm.

   This helps expand your lung capacity and also helps train you to use your diaphragm to control your breath as you're speaking.

6. Repeat the sequence 3-5 times.

Mah, Maw, Mah Scales

For these next workouts you'll be saying the syllables Mah, Maw, Mah, and other sounds on a musical scale.[1] Do them gently, the sound does not need to be loud for the workouts to be effective.

1. Stand comfortably, legs slightly apart.

2. Inhale diaphragmatically. Remember, your shoulders are down and relaxed.

---

[1] A scale is a series of notes or tones that divide an octave, twelve notes in Western music.

3. Exhale as you say Mah, Maw, Mah, on one breath. Doing this will be like singing the notes. Begin on any note that is comfortable for you.

   The 'aw' and 'ah' sounds should feel as if they're in the same place as the 'm' sound: at the front of your lips.

   Try to extend the last word, Mah, so it sounds like Maaaaah.

4. Once you've exhaled, inhale and repeat #3.

5. Continue doing this workout, starting a note higher as long as you are comfortable and are not straining each time. Your throat should feel relaxed, and you should be breathing diaphragmatically. When you reach he highest note at which you are comfortable:

6. Say the same syllables: Mah, Maw, Mah, but now go down the scale.

Do the workout, going up and down the scale, as far as your range allows. If you can only do a few notes up and down, that's fine. As you work, you may discover that your vocal range begins expanding.

Mah, May, Me, Moh, Moo Scales

Follow the instructions for the Mah, Maw, Mah scales, but replace the Mah, Maw, Mah sounds with: Mah, May, Me, Moh, Moo.

Use these and the diaphragmatic breathing workouts on a daily basis. The freedom, vocal stamina and flexibility they'll give you will power your voice for your storytelling.

PART TWO

THE NARRATIVE

Every book's story is told by its book narrator. It is his or her voice, also called The Narrative Voice, that conveys not merely the content, but the heart of that story. And for as long as the story lasts, you and that book narrator are one. How you interpret the story is how he or she interprets it.

This Narrative Voice is not a physical one but an emotional, intellectual one. It expresses the tone of the story and the point of view of the book narrator. Tone and point of view are deeply connected; they are two key strands of audiobook DNA. We're going to tease them apart temporarily to help give you mastery over each.

Tone is where we begin.

3

Tone

Don't use that tone with me.

—Everybody's mother

S arcastic, rebellious, secretive, aggressive, impertinent; our mothers didn't have to see the look on our faces to know what we were feeling. We could have been speaking gibberish and they would have understood, because it was right there in our tone—the emotion and attitude we were conveying.

Research has shown that the brain is affected—positively or negatively—by tone from birth.[1] This built-in receptivity to tone allows us to convey our thoughts, our feelings and our attitudes far more decisively than can words alone. 'I love you,' said in a romantic tone can melt the listener. But 'I love you?' said in a mocking, derisive tone can leave that listener sobbing and reaching for another piece of chocolate.

---

[1] Y. Saito, S. Aoyama, T. Kondo, R. Fukumoto, N. Konishi, K. Nakamura, M. Kobayashi, T. Toshima, "Frontal Cerebral Blood Flow Change Associated with Infant-Drected Speech." BMJ Publishing Group & Royal College of Paediatrics and Child Health, 2007.

The tone you establish for a book sets the stage upon which the story unfolds. It establishes the book's mood, its emotional atmosphere. We recognize the importance of tone in film and on stage e.g.: dark, gloomy, bright, romantic, comedic, etc. But what a director creates with lights, angles, color, set, sound effects, music and cast, you have the power to create with just your voice and your imagination. And the first step to giving the text a tone is to personally connect to the story.

A. Connecting to the Story

Connecting to the story means allowing its words and events to ignite your emotional and imaginative responses to it.

Three simple techniques are particularly effective in facilitating this connection.

Read Aloud

You can understand a book while reading silently, but speaking the words aloud is transformative; it increases your ability to recognize and give voice to moments, ideas and reactions that might slip past you if you read silently. And it gives you a greater facility with the language of the story so that you will read with fewer mistakes when you're ready to record.

I worked with an experienced actor who clearly hadn't bothered to read the manuscript aloud before our session. He was starring in a hit TV show and was beyond smug. His initial, 'I can do this with my eyes closed' approach quickly crumbled as he began stumbling through the text from the very first page. The poor guy was unable to get through a paragraph because it had no meaning for him, it was just a bunch of words. He'd get confused about what he was reading, stumble, mispronounce words and have to stop and start again. He had to do this several times on nearly every page during the reading, turning our studio time into a rehearsal. What should have been an enjoyable six-hour recording session, turned into sixteen hours of torture! The exhausted engineer kept sliding lower and lower in his seat until I had to practically yank him up from under the console. I downed about seventy-five cups of coffee, and the mortified actor was, by hour two, cursing at himself and apologizing to us at every turn of a page. I tried to make him feel better, assuring him that everyone makes mistakes, but the truth is, if he'd read the manuscript aloud, he'd have had a much better experience and outcome.

Slow it Down

Read at a slower pace than you normally would. Give yourself time for whatever response is emerging to rise to the surface. Give yourself the time – and the freedom—to discover the personal connections you have to the language and ideas in the story you are reading. New actors are especially surprised at how by merely slowing down their reading, unexpected reactions emerge, creating a more individual and exciting performance.

Do Nothing

Do Nothing is an active approach that means don't apply a preconceived notion of how a story should be read. Instead, at this stage, do nothing to stop your subconscious from bringing up its unexpected insights, emotions and ideas. Trust yourself. You will respond. You will react. You will find connections to the text.

The technique of Do Nothing is especially important for new audiobook actors and for those times when you're reading material that you're having difficulty connecting to. Doing nothing can quickly yield a lot of 'somethings' because that's when sparks fly; that's when insightful, original reactions emerge because they are not being crowded out by what you think you should be doing. That's when the experiences of your life, your particular way of looking at the world—what makes you laugh, what touches you, what you think is important, powerful, worthy of note, worthy of scorn, worthy of excitement—get expressed.

Using these three simple techniques will pay off when you get to your recording session. You won't be spending sixteen hours on a six-hour production. You wouldn't go onstage without rehearsal—the same holds for audiobook acting, and connecting to the story is the first step in your preparation.

Connecting to the Story Workouts

The following short stories are structured to allow you to discover your personal responses to them. For now, don't analyze the story; don't try to get it right. Just allow yourself to respond.

Remember, put your three techniques to work:

> Read Aloud
> Slow it Down
> Do Nothing

If you find that you're imposing a concept of how a story should be read, stop. Relax. A few breathing exercises will help you get out of your head. Then start again.

Read the story a few times until you feel you're personally connecting to it. Don't try to repeat how you read it the time before. Your original responses may still be there, but new ones may also come up. Let that happen. It can be surprising how much more emerges when you read the text again.

In audiobook acting, as previously noted, you will play all the characters. So everyone should read all the stories no matter the gender, age, ethnicity or nationality of the characters featured.

Text: JOHN

John is always late. Make a three o'clock appointment with him and you'd be an idiot to show up until at least four. He says he isn't doing it on purpose. He's not trying to make a statement; he just can't help himself. He blames it on his mother because he says that she always kept him waiting as a child. He blames it on his dad, his brother, his sister, anyone in his past whom he knows won't protest too much. Of course, he's twenty-four now, and this all happened in his childhood, at least according to him, and he could try to be on time now. But no matter what you say, no matter how much you beg or plead or cajole, he will be late. He's even late for his own events. He threw a birthday party for himself with the invite clearly stating 8 p.m.

He didn't show till nine.

After you've read the JOHN story a few times, take a moment to think about what you experienced. Did the story make you laugh? Did you find John likeable? Funny? Weird? Quirky? Did you perhaps stretch the words, 'anyone in his past' as you said them, giving them a little bit of humor or light sarcasm? Did you find yourself metaphorically rolling your eyes as you read that John 'didn't show till nine?' Conversely, maybe you felt annoyed at John and sneered on the words, 'he's not trying to make a statement.' Perhaps you thought John had a lot of nerve and when you reached the end of the story, you were irritated by his lack of concern for others.

There are no right or wrong responses at this point. The purpose of these early workouts is to allow you to discover how you personally connect with the text, what you bring to it.

Audiobook Acting is an art, and the more you allow yourself the freedom to be responsive, the more honest and interesting your reading will be for both you and the listener.

You're in the arts because you have something to express. Don't limit yourself.

Apply the three techniques to the following selection.

Text: JANICE

Janice sat at the edge of the hill directly behind the garden. The land was flat for fifty feet and then there was a sharp upturn creating the impression of a miniature mountain rather than a hill. It boasted some small, squat shrubs that leaned out from the incline as if in search of sun. She needed to sit there, up against a hill she couldn't climb—a hill that led nowhere—as if it was the only place she deserved. She found it comforting somehow: the earth, the small plants struggling for light just as she was. They too were silent, non-complaining and perhaps, she thought, they too were aware that they would never do more than cling to the side of this hill.

The phone was ringing in the house. She longed to get up, to see who was calling. She longed for someone or something to reach out to her. But she was weary, too weary in that moment to even stand. She watched a tiny plant, leaves open in expectation. Then she held her breath until the ringing stopped.

How did the story affect you? Did you feel tenderness or perhaps sadness when reading? Did your voice grow quieter as you read about Janice's self-imposed silence? Did you feel compassion for her? Did you discover a note of hopefulness at any point, or did you react critically, feeling uncomfortable at her withdrawal? Did you pull back? Judge her?

If you didn't have any reactions to the story, go back and read it again until you do.

In the next story, a big city guy, Mike, is looking for a change in his life. Again, you don't have to be the same gender as the book narrator or lead character to do this or any of the workouts. You just have to connect to the story.

Text: THE EXISTENTIAL COWBOY

After Woodstock, when Mike decided to move to Miami from New York City, he'd bought an apartment in what was then the swingin'est private club around, The Jockey Club. There were loads of wealthy members, including a bunch of single women, mostly rich divorcees looking to reconnect. He was twenty-nine, fairly good-looking, with a few bucks in his jeans. He drove a Porsche then; life was good. But after a few years of that lifestyle, he began to resent having to wear a suit every day, resent the traffic between home and office and resent the thorough urbanization of Miami. He knew he wanted a change. But to what?

He'd always loved all things Western. His favorite movies were Westerns. His childhood fantasy had been to be a cowboy. As a kid he'd dress up and buckle on a holster, fill it with his .45 cap gun, and practice his quick draw for hours in front of his mom's full-length mirror. That had to stop when he lost control once: the gun went flying out of his hand, scratching the mirror pretty badly. So he thought Why not? Why not investigate? Check it out? If not now, when?

Forty-five minutes out of Miami was an area of horse and cattle ranches surrounding a small town called Davie that had a rodeo arena, feed store, and a country and western saloon. It was a place where instead of driving, people rode their horses to town.

He'd let go of the memories of Manhattan and his life in Miami, jump in the Porsche and head out there. It would be the beginning of his transformation.[1]

What emerged in your reading? What did you feel and express? Your reactions are the foundation of establishing the tone of a story.

---

[1] Text THE EXISTENTIAL COWBOY by Ira Marks.

Once you are comfortable with the first step—personally connecting with the story—the second step is to identify the tone your reactions give rise to.

B. Identify the Tone

This means recognizing and naming the overall tone that your reading expresses, e.g., wry, adventurous, tender, yearning, reverential, humorous, etc. Sometimes the exact tonal word comes to you easily, but if it doesn't, if you can't identify the tone your responses reflect, here's a tool that can help.

Note It

Make a note of the images, ideas and feelings that come to you right at the place in the text where they occur. You can do it as you're reading or afterward. You don't have to make a note of everything that comes to you, just what is especially meaningful. Writing the word(s) reinforces the thought(s) in your brain. And notes are nifty little reminders of that great inspiration you had if you need to jog your memory.

Perhaps when working on THE EXISTENTIAL COWBOY, saying 'the swingin'est club' reminded you of a club you loved to hang out in, or a club you read about that was hot or cool, so you said the words with relish or a little swagger. Maybe the word 'cowboy' made you laugh or evoked a feeling of tenderness for the child you were, or it brought back the image of you in that crazy photo when you were a kid with a ten-gallon hat on a two-gallon head. Maybe you said the words 'life was good' with affection or a sigh of satisfaction; or maybe you said them with a touch of regret, implying that life just wasn't good enough. The words 'horse and cattle ranches' might have made you feel inspired, remembering when you wanted open spaces, and you gave them some pizzaz, or you lingered on those words. Note those reactions.

Once you've noted your responses, review those notes and name the tone they indicate. Don't worry if you change your mind later on. That's what erasers are for—or the delete button.

Identify the Tone Workouts

Re-read THE EXISTENTIAL COWBOY and note your emotional responses as they occur.

Text: THE EXISTENTIAL COWBOY

After Woodstock, when Mike decided to move to Miami from New York City, he'd bought an apartment in what was then the swingin'est private club around, The Jockey Club. There were loads of wealthy members, including a bunch of single women, mostly rich divorcees looking to reconnect. He was twenty-nine, fairly good-looking, with a few bucks in his jeans. He drove a Porsche then; life was good. But after a few years of that lifestyle, he began to resent having to wear a suit every day, resent the traffic between home and office and resent the thorough urbanization of Miami. He knew he wanted a change. But to what?

He'd always loved all things Western. His favorite movies were Westerns. His childhood fantasy had been to be a cowboy. As a kid he'd dress up and buckle on a holster, fill it with his .45 cap gun, and practice his quick draw for hours in front of his mom's full-length mirror. That had to stop when he lost control once: the gun went flying out of his hand, scratching the mirror pretty badly. So he thought Why not? Why not investigate? Check it out? If not now, when?

Forty-five minutes out of Miami was an area of horse and cattle ranches surrounding a small town called Davie that had a rodeo arena, feed store, and a country and western saloon. It was a place where instead of driving, people rode their horses to town.

He'd let go of the memories of Manhattan and his life in Miami, jump in the Porsche and head out there. It would be the beginning of his transformation.[1]

---

[1] Text THE EXISTENTIAL COWBOY by Ira Marks.

Here's THE EXISTENTIAL COWBOY with some examples of notes.

Text: THE EXISTENTIAL COWBOY (with notes)

After Woodstock, when Mike decided to move to Miami from New York City, he'd bought an apartment in what was then the swingin'est *MAD FUN* private club around, The Jockey Club. There were loads of wealthy members including a bunch of single women, mostly rich divorcees *HOT* looking to reconnect. He was twenty-nine, fairly good-looking, with a few bucks in his jeans. He drove a Porsche *BRAG* then; life was good. But after a few years of that lifestyle, he began to resent having to wear a suit every day, *REALIZATION* resent the traffic between home and office and resent the thorough urbanization *TOSS IT* of Miami. He knew he wanted a change. But *PROBE* to what?

He'd always loved all things Western. *REALIZATION* His favorite movies were Westerns. His childhood fantasy had been to be a cowboy. *LAUGH* As a kid he'd dress up and buckle on a holster, *ENJOY* fill it with his .45 cap gun and practice his quick draw for hours in front of his mom's full-length mirror. That had to stop when he lost control once, *LAUGH* the gun flying out of his hand, scratching the mirror pretty badly. So, he thought Why not? *EXCITED* Why not investigate? Check it out? *MORE EXCITED* If not now, he thought, when?

Forty-five minutes out of Miami was an area of horse and cattle ranches surrounding a small town called Davie that had a rodeo arena, feed store, and a country and western saloon. It was a place where instead of driving, people rode their horses to town.

He'd let go of the memories of Manhattan and his life in Miami, jump in the Porsche *EMBRACE IT* and head out there. It would be the beginning of his transformation.

Based on those notes, one actor might decide the tone was *exuber-ant*. Another actor might identify the tone as *optimistic* or *champing at the bit* or *zesty*. Maybe another would call it *empowering*. All of those tone-defining words would be appropriate given those notes. You will likely come up with a very different set of responses and tone.

Let's return to the JOHN story. Read it again and identify the tone you are using. Note your responses as you go.

Text: JOHN

John is always late. Make a three o'clock appointment with him and you'd be an idiot to show up until at least four. He says he isn't doing it on purpose. He's not trying to make a statement; he just can't help himself. He blames it on his mother because he says that she always kept him waiting as a child. He blames it on his dad, his brother, his sister, anyone in his past whom he knows won't protest too much. Of course, he's twenty-four now, and this all happened in his childhood, at least according to him, and he could try to be on time now. But no matter what you say, no matter how much you beg or plead or cajole, he will be late. He's even late for his own events. He threw a birthday party for himself with the invite clearly stating 8 p.m.

He didn't show till nine.

What tone emerged? Was it *amused*? Was it disdainful or *contemp-tuous*? Was it *smug*? *Sympathetic*? *Sarcastic*? Remember, there is no right or wrong at this point in the work. You are focusing on allowing your responses to emerge and thus connect you to the story.

Whatever tone you come up with creates the atmosphere of the story. And it creates a picture of the character referred to. If your tone is *amused* in the JOHN story, you'll convey the idea that John is a quirky character who, despite his perennial lateness, is still a good guy. You might laugh at his foibles as you describe them, and the listener will get the idea that he is funny or endearing. Alternately, if your tone is *disdainful*, the listener will see John as a selfish, inconsiderate man who cares little for others' needs, and the tone of the story won't be *funny*, but *critical*.

Of course, actors know you can't 'play a tone;' you can't play an emotion or a state of being. But that is not what you'll be doing. By identifying a tone, you will make instinctive choices that are active; you'll do something. If your tone is *amused*, for example, you might laugh at John's behavior, you might tease or brush it off in your reading. If your tone is *dismissive*, you might mock him, belittle him, or maybe scoff during your reading.

You'd go crazy if you read an entire book consciously picking and choosing how to read every word or sentence. You don't have to. The tone you choose at the beginning, sets the emotional foundation for your reading.

Once you've connected to the story and identified its tone, the third step is to apply it.

C. Apply the Tone

You apply the tone by simply keeping it in mind as you begin reading the story. If, for example, the tone you came up with for THE EXISTENTIAL COWBOY was *exciting*, keep the word *exciting* in mind as you read. You don't have to be big, you don't have to whoop and holler, you don't have to do anything but keep the word *exciting* in your mind. We just have to think of excitement and our whole system responds; we feel an uplift, a vibrancy, a positive energy which is then expressed in our reading.

Commit to the tone you are working with. Commitment is a powerful thing. When you commit to a tone, you will focus on the story itself and not on whether you are right or wrong. And that's when wonderful, unexpected inspiration occurs!

Sometimes the tone you've chosen can surprise you. Maybe you think the tone you've identified, though it feels right, is wrong. Before you judge yourself, try it out. Too often self-criticism can damper creativity so Welcome the Unexpected. One actor was not thrilled with the tone he'd identified for a book we were beginning to work on. The tone he'd come up with was *arrogant*. It was an unexpected choice for the material, and he said, "I think that's wrong." I urged him to apply it anyway. "There's no right or wrong at this stage. Test it and see what happens." He began reading with *arrogant* as the tone, and his reading was vibrant and illuminated the text in an unanticipated, but very interesting way.

As you begin the following workouts, remember:

Read Aloud
Slow it Down
Do Nothing
Note It
Welcome the Unexpected

Apply the Tone/Fiction Workouts

Read the next story, DEAD CAT, until you can identify the tone you are giving it. Then read it again, this time applying the tone by keeping it in mind as you read.

Text: DEAD CAT

I'm riding on a New York City subway car with a dead cat in my backpack. I have it wrapped in a plastic grocery bag inside a shoe box. I'm hoping that will keep it from reeking too badly until I get to Manhattan, but I'm kind of paranoid that it won't.

The car I'm in is uncrowded, not unusual for a night in August. This allows me to keep a distance between myself and the other passengers, lessening my fear of detection by odor. The cool of the air-conditioned car is a welcome relief from the stifling heat outside, and the rhythmical clacking of the train wheels rolling over the tracks has a calming effect on my brain, putting me in a near meditative state. As I sit here with the backpack/cadaver between my feet, my mind drifts to the cause of this ludicrous situation, my ex: Regan. We recently broke up after sixteen spiteful years together. Our relationship was never good, her being a hateful bitch and all. But I guess after being raised by a bipolar, pill head mom, she has reason to be.

I knew she wasn't right in the head going in. But I had a foolproof strategy guaranteed to fix her, the healing power of love. My love was sure to wipe out the lifetime of horror she suffered. If I just hung in there long enough, put up with enough of her insanity and bullshit, the real Regan would emerge—kind, loving, forgiving. But my brilliant plan failed. The tender, compassionate Regan never showed herself. My only reward for sixteen years of torture was a lunatic, hell-bent on disemboweling my ego.

So, I got out. I had to get free. But if I'm really free, then why am I riding on a New York City subway car with a dead cat between my feet just because she told me to? Why does she still have this controlling effect on me? And why, after years of fighting and six months of separation, do I still love her? I have to figure this one out soon, or my heart will be slave to her forever.[1]

The DEAD CAT story is full of tonal possibilities: *sarcastic, comic, irreverent, self-deprecatory, wistful, introspective, depressed* and *yearning* are just a few examples.

---

[1] Text DEAD CAT by Neil Mitchell

As you re-read a story, you may have new and different responses to it. The more you dig in, the more you'll dig up. And if your reactions change, your tone may change. Those changes, those fresh insights, make your reading richer and multi-layered.

All of the material we've been working with reads as fiction. We're now going to turn to a nonfiction text. People sometimes think that they've got to give nonfiction work a more formal, 'just the facts' performance. That can undermine the power of the book and its message. The author wrote it because they were passionate about the topic, or felt the urgency of conveying their information, or they were inspired by the material or felt their discovery was a rollicking adventure. Applying the techniques you've been using for fiction to nonfiction, enables you to connect to a tone that will convey that passion, urgency, or inspiration, and be a catalyst for the listener's emotions and interest.

Apply the Tone/Nonfiction Workouts

Apply all your techniques to the next text, THE ARBITRATION, and see what tone emerges. Note your responses for this workout.

Text: THE ARBITRATION

As our arbitration slogged on, I began to see it in broader terms than just our problem. It was a problem with the legal system. Our defendant perjured himself in court documents to an astounding level. And when we discussed whether this was actionable, most lawyers laughed. "Everybody lies. Forget about it. No one cares. Get on with your life."

This was not always so. In the past, there were significant punishments for Civil Perjury, for the courts recognized the damage such acts do to the litigants and the very system itself. They recognized that granting a free pass to those who lie in an effort to 'legally steal' would ultimately create a distrust and disrespect for the system that stands at the center of our civil society. They understood that false affidavits and false testimony waste the resources of the courts and the arbitration system and create huge amounts of unnecessary legal fees and delays.

Judges and arbitrators are at the root of the problem by allowing perjury as Standard Operating Procedure. If perjury is no big deal, a non-event, why not lie? After all, nothing will be done. There will be no consequences and without consequences, for many the law is irrelevant. Though Civil Perjury is legally deemed a crime with fines and imprisonment, it is most often met with no punishment.

How did you react? Did you feel passionate about the issue? Did you feel dismayed by the information? Did you feel angry at the system? Did you find any ironic moments? What tone did your reading produce? Some actors prefer to use simple words to identify their reactions, but you should write whatever notes reflect your responses and get your creativity going. Here is a sample response to the text.

Text: THE ARBITRATION (with notes)

As our arbitration slogged on, I began to see it in broader terms than just our problem. *ANNOYED* It was a problem with the legal system. Our defendant perjured himself in court documents to an astounding level. And when we discussed whether this was actionable, most lawyers laughed. "Everybody lies. *TOSS OFF* Forget about it. No one cares. Get on with your life."

This was not always so. *CLARIFY* In the past there were significant punishments for Civil Perjury, for the courts recognized the damage such acts do to the litigants and the very system itself. They recognized that by granting a free pass to those who lie in an effort to *EMPHASIZE* 'legally steal' would ultimately create a distrust and disrespect for the system that stands at the center of our civil society. *BE CLEAR* They understood that false affidavits and false testimony waste the resources of the courts and the arbitration system and create huge amounts of unnecessary legal fees and delays.

Judges and arbitrators *ACCUSE* are at the root of the problem by allowing perjury as Standard Operating Procedure. *NAIL IT* If perjury is no big deal, a non-event, why not lie? After all, nothing will be done. There will be no consequences and *PROSECUTE* without consequences, for many the law is irrelevant. Though Civil Perjury is legally deemed a crime with fines and imprisonment, it is most often met with no punishment.

The tone emerging from those notes might be *accusative*. Or it might be *contemptuous, angry*, or *snide* for example.

It bears repeating: naming a tone doesn't constrict or limit you; it gives you a framework for your reading. You can express many different emotions as the story progresses, you'll just express them within that framework. If a young hero gets depressed in a book that is an ironic comedy, he won't get depressed as if he's the protagonist in a dystopian novel. You'll make him ironically depressed or comedically depressed. If you've decided the tone of a book is a *frothy romp*, you won't make your frothy heroine suddenly sound as if she's in a Greek tragedy when she gets angry. She'll be frothily angry, or frothily irate, or frothily indignant. Don't limit yourself. There are lots of ways to froth!

As you become more and more adept at connecting to the text, keep this next technique in mind.

Don't Overdo It

Your performance is most often being heard by one person at a time through headphones or a speaker. This creates a very direct connection between you and the listener. Big dramatics sound overblown and forced on audio. Just as a camera captures the slightest flicker of emotion on an actor's face, the microphone conveys your thoughts and emotional responses without the need for you to push it. Record yourself as you read these workouts. Singers always listen to their takes, why not you? Record whatever text you are working with. Let a little time go by, then listen to it. Do you hear the book narrator telling the story directly to you, or does it sound like a reading for a larger audience? As you get used to the contained dynamics of audiobook performing, you'll be able to quickly assess when you're too big, too small or right in the Goldilocks spot.

In the prior sections, you've been working to explore your responses to a story without making any judgements about being right or wrong and with no preconceived idea of what the story's tone should be. But there are times when the tone has been defined.

D. Working with a Defined Tone

A publisher may define the book's tone when assigning a production to an actor. They'll say: It's a *wistful* memoir about an expat's sojourn in India, or,

- ◆ A wry look at university life.

- ◆ A tender family memoir.

- ◆ A harsh look at the effects of climate change.

- ◆ A humorous take on modern romance.

- ◆ A tension-filled adventure story.

Using a defined tone doesn't mean you force yourself into a predictable read. It just means that you begin with that tone in mind. You still do your responsive work because your interpretation of the defined tone will be unique to you. Your *wistful* or *wry* or *harsh* tone will be different from that of every other actor.

Defined Tone Workouts

Let's assume your publisher described the following story as 'a sympathetic portrait of a boy on the edge.' The tone they want is *sympathetic*. Read aloud and slow it down to allow time for things to bubble up. Don't try to decide what a *sympathetic* tone should sound like. Do nothing but keep the tone in mind.

Text: THE KID

The kid stood off to the side of the playground, eyes to the ground. He was perhaps twelve or thirteen. One toe pushed at the dirt in front of him as if he was trying to appear engaged in thought and not attract any attention. He avoided eye contact holding his jacket tight against the cold. His hands were shoved deep into his pockets. He was detached, strange, clearly a loner. The question was why?

Perhaps the image of the boy standing in the playground alone, without friends, made you feel *concerned* about him. Perhaps you felt an unexpected *tenderness* toward him. Or perhaps the image of him holding his jacket tight against the cold night made you feel *protective*. Any of those responses—*concerned, tender* or *protective*—are perfect tonal words that would be compatible with the publisher's defined *sympathetic* tone.

Let's switch it up. Let's say the publisher instead said that the story was a 'tough look at marginal youth.' Read the text again, but this time keep the *tough* tone in mind.

One student working with the *tough* tone had a really interesting response. She said that as she read, she suddenly felt that the boy might be a dangerous person, someone she should watch out for, and she was steeling herself against the possibility of something perilous to come. Fleeting moments of tension and wariness came up in her reading and the tone she gave the story changed from the defined *tough* to *guarded*.

Because the tone she began with was *tough*, her *guarded* tone didn't become fearful, or sensitive, it was wary, watchful and strong, and she created a multi-layered, compelling reading.

Another student had a similar experience when given a defined tone for a different story. This gentleman is a professional fund-raiser and a grandfather. He's got a terrific voice, loves to read to his grandkids and wanted to check out audiobook acting as a second, albeit late-stage, career. We began with a children's book he'd brought with him. It was about an animal, and his reading started off with a typical singsong approach—up and down, up and down, very boring, very uninteresting. Unless he'd held his grandkids in a firm grip as he read, I think the kids would have scooted away.

So, I stopped him and gave him a defined tone. I asked him to slow down and do nothing but keep a *playful* tone in mind.

He began again, reading slowly. But this time, he suddenly paused after one line to create suspense and anticipation, and then he leapt forward with glee to the next. He began playing with the words, making some sound funny and others goofy. He started creating tiny dramas in a single line. Those reactions were totally unplanned. They happened because he slowed down and just kept *playful* in mind. It transformed his reading; it became imaginative, engaging and organic. As he worked with the *playful* tone, he got even more imaginative and daring. When he finished, I asked whether his tone was still *playful*. He thought for a minute and said, "No. It was *silly!*"

"Read it again," I said, "and this time, keep *silly* in mind as the tone." *Silly* was perfect, and it brought the magic out of him.

Following is an excerpt from a poetic version of the fairy tale, "Rapunzel," written for kids. The story is about seclusion, revenge and finally, later, a happy ending. This version has a lot of opportunities for fun, so start with the defined tone *playful*. Keep that in mind and see what emerges.

You don't have to read the poem in a regular meter. It is written with very little punctuation so that you can feel free in your reading. You can stretch words, slow them down, speed them up, let yourself screech, growl and play.

Text: RAP, RAP, RAP, RAPUNZEL

Once upon a time, long ago
Before there was TV or radio
In a far-away land, across the sea
Lived a man and his wife who were happy as could be
Livin' in a forest that was deep and green
In the sweetest little cottage you have ever seen
And best of all, in a little while
The husband and the wife were gonna have a child

Now next to their cottage was a garden full
Of every single type of yummy vegetable
But one called the rampion was the veggie queen
It had vitamins and minerals and it was leafy and green

Now this garden had a wall that was high and wide
And no one dared to go inside
'Cause it belonged to a witch of great power
A witch who grew stronger with every hour
A sorceress of magic and mystery
She knew all the secrets of history
She had ancient spells and frightening looks
Magical charms she found in her books
She could turn a hippo into a rat
Turn a bug upside down, make it hang like a bat
Turn a boy into a lizard
She was such a scary wizard
And the garden had a sign
KEEP OUT ITS MINE!!!

Did you find your *playful* tone? Did it stay *playful* or become *silly*, or *silly scary*, or *slap-happy* or any other word that allowed you to capture the playfulness of the poem?

Here's a technique that can help if you get stuck:

Read as if to Someone You Know

Consider this an adjunct technique. You may not have to use it, but it can be helpful if you feel you aren't connecting to the material. Visualize yourself reading to someone you know well and whose responses to ideas or attitudes you are familiar with. For example, you know how your family members or close friends react to things, so make one of them your 'listener.' You can easily imagine—see—their responses as you read the story. If your listener looks interested, you may emphasize a point; you may play with the language. If her attention drifts, you may read in a quieter voice to get her to pay more attention to the story, or you might make your reading scarier or more intense. If you see her nodding in agreement, you might emphasize those lines even more strongly. If she starts to smile, you may up your game to make her giggle.

Stage and film actors rehearse scenes and monologues using this technique and it's easily adaptable to audiobooks.

One aspiring audiobook actor worked on the "Rapunzel" poem and read it the first time in a very dull manner. So, I gave him the same defined tone of *playful* and asked him to read it as if telling the story to one of his kids. This was a different person than the grandfather, but the results were similar. Unexpectedly, he found himself making crazy voices, escalating the tension on some sentences, soaring a line upward on certain words and then dropping his voice to a squeaky scared whisper on others. He gave himself time to allow his responses to emerge as he imagined the child's reactions—her eyes growing bigger at one point, her giggles at another. Those imagined reactions encouraged more responses in him. He was totally surprised when all this emerged. He had allowed himself to be free and to feel; he had imagined his child's reactions and the result was fabulous. His eyes lit up and he became very excited. Afterwards, he said he felt as if he'd been flying. The original *playful* tone morphed into a tone he called *rollicking*, and if he had actually been reading to his child, I think she'd have been glued to every word, just as I was.

Here's the "Rapunzel" poem with notes by that aspiring actor. He'd read it a few times, making some notes as he went along, using the *playful* tone. By the last read, he never referred to the notes; he was 'in the zone,' connected, expressive, and creating a one of a kind read.

Text: RAP, RAP, RAP, RAPUNZEL (with notes)

Once upon a time, long *STRETCH WORDS* ago
Before there was TV or radio
In a faraway land, across the sea
Lived a man and his wife who were happy *SILLY* as could be
Livin' in a forest that was deep *LOW* and green
In the sweetest little cottage you have ever seen
And best of all, *PAUSE* in a little while
The husband and the wife were gonna have a child
Now next to their cottage was a garden full
Of every single type of yummy vegetable
But one called the rampion was the veggie queen
It had vitamins and minerals and it was leafy and green

Now this garden had a wall that was high and wide
And no one ever dared to go inside.
'Cause it belonged to a witch slow *EMPHASIZE* of great power
A witch who grew stronger with every hour
A sorceress of magic and mystery *SCARY*
She knew *WAVERY VOICE* all the secrets of history
She had ancient spells and frightening looks
Magical charms that she found in her books

She could *SCARED* turn a hippo into a rat *LOUDER*
Turn a bug upside down, make it hang like a bat *LOUDER*
Turn a boy into a lizard,
She was such a scary wizard
And the garden had a sign
KEEP OUT *LOUD, GRUFF*
IT'S MINE!!! *EXTENDED GROWL*

The "Rapunzel" poem might have been equally well read by someone whose tone was *whimsical,* or *scary magical,* or *whacky, zany,* or *tickly.* Use whatever word that makes it work for you. *Blungababble* is fine if it gets your creative juices going.

Let's try a defined tone on a nonfiction text.

Begin reading the following as though the publisher's defined tone was *scholarly.* That would be a loosely defined tone, with a lot of possibilities. Don't get stuck thinking scholarly has to be cold or unemotional. Your approach to *scholarly* could be *cool* or *wise,* or it might be *engaging,* or *compelling* or *passionate* or *humorous* for example. Be sure to convey the information clearly and see what happens when you begin reading with *scholarly* in mind.

Text: BEING HUMAN

Homo sapiens' ability to create, understand and respond to symbols was thought to be the hallmark of our species, an ability shared by no others including the Neanderthals, who became extinct about 40,000 years ago. Cave art, a powerful demonstration of symbolic culture, was assumed to have been created only by our modern human ancestors.

Neanderthals have long been considered to be, and portrayed as, brutish and cognitively deficient. But current technology is changing that view. Based on the geochronological dating method—Uranium-thorium dating—done at three sites in

Spain, scholars have dated several episodes of cave painting back as far as 66,700 years. According to Chris Standish and Alistair Pike in their article, "How We Discovered that Neanderthals Could Make Art," the results "demonstrate that cave art was being created in all three sites at least 20,000 years prior to the arrival of Homo sapiens in Europe."[1] That information has powerful implications for our understanding of what it means to be human.

Someone who loves anthropology might see this story as *illuminating* or *compelling*. They might see it as *inspirational* or *galvanizing*. Another person, who has long fought against the view of Neanderthals as merely brutish, might see this as a moment of *triumph*, or as one of *justification*. Our reactions to a story emerge from how we see the events and ideas in it. And that brings us to the other strand of Audio DNA: the book narrator's Point of View.

---

[1] Chris Standish, Alistair Pike, "How We Discovered that Neanderthals Could Make Art." theconversation.com, February, 2018.

4

Point of View (POV)

Try to see it my way...
—Lennon-McCartney

Point of View in literary analysis refers to whether a story is told in first, second, or third person. For the audiobook actor, point of view also means the lens through which the book narrator views the story—how he or she sees and interprets the events, emotions, ideas, etc.

Since you are doing the reading, as noted earlier, for as long as the story lasts, you and the book narrator are one and the same. How you express things is how the book narrator expresses things. How you react to the events is how he or she reacts.

I also noted that tone and point of view are two strands of audiobook DNA. They are intimately connected because as you define the tone of a text, you are simultaneously giving the book narrator a point of view. If the RAP, RAP, RAP, RAPUNZEL poem has a *playful* tone, it means your book narrator is someone from whose point of view the poem is fun and who has a playful personality. The tale of a cruel witch who, the story eventually reveals, locks poor Rapunzel away in a tower, could be the stuff of nightmares, but not if your book narrator sees it as a zany romp in a fairy tale forest, a story told by a fun-loving book narrator.

If your tone in the DEAD CAT story was *ironic*, then in your hands the book narrator is someone with an ironic point of view about life, someone who sees things from under an arched eyebrow, lightly mocking everything, including him or herself. The way we see things is greatly a function of our personality. A person with a sunny, optimistic personality will usually see things from a positive point of view. Things that would bother the pessimist might be laughed away by the optimist.

While tone is a great entry point into a book, the point of view may be what you connect to first. Understanding how to work from both access points gives you flexibility and greater command over any book you're asked to read.

Some actors I've directed were initially wary of working with a point of view and tone, saying they didn't want to impose their interpretation on the listener. But imagine going to see a play in which the actors didn't 'impose their interpretations' on the audience. You would be bored to tears by the end of the first scene, and asleep or gone, by the second.

Audiobook acting is a dramatic art. Your interpretation is key to the experience.

Reading a story without giving it a point of view and tone just sounds like reciting a bunch of disconnected statements: "so then I said and he said and she said and they said and I said and the sun rose and the car broke down and the fish were in the water and we walked up the hill."

That was my experience with one well-known actor I was directing. Her reading was flat and dull, but she was haughtily resistant to any direction. We in the control room were mighty bored. My engineer was doodling on his script! A very bad sign.

So at one extremely snore-inducing point in the session, I ever-so-delicately suggested a point of view. It was something I felt she could handle because it was right for the book, and she was a very experienced actor. I urged her to give it a try. She was reluctant. "It would be," she protested, "too much! Over the top!"

"You can be subtle," I responded. "I'm not suggesting grand theatrics." Still, she was resistant.

"Try it for this one section," I said. "You can listen to the playbacks of your previous read and the new one. You can pick which you prefer and that's the one I'll use."

"I know how you directors are," she huffed. "You say that now, but you'll use whatever you like when you edit."

"Noooo," I said as my engineer shook his head and doodled away. "You can come into the control room to listen with us, and we'll delete the take you don't like right in front of you."

She finally agreed to try it. She read from the point of view I'd suggested. When she finished reading, she got up from her seat, flounced out of the recording booth and came into the control room to listen. She could have listened in the recording booth, but she clearly wanted to be sure I deleted the take she didn't like.

The engineer played both takes. They were like night and day. The one with the point of view gave the reading meaning and focus. It danced on the ear. The other one was like gears grinding.

I knew it, the engineer knew it, and so did that actor!

We waited for her response.

She stared at the wall for a minute.

"Okay," she finally muttered, as if she was doing me a favor. "Just use the take you like!" And out she flounced. When we began recording again, she continued giving the book the point of view we'd tried. The reading was now interesting and engaging. It now had a point of view. It had a tone. My engineer gave me a thumbs up and stopped doodling. I was really pleased and assumed the actor felt good about the improvement.

My engineer called me a few days later while he was editing the program. "Listen to this," he said laughing. "She obviously didn't realize the mic was on before she began reading again." He turned up the volume on the speakers. I suddenly heard her cursing me under her breath.

No question what her point of view was about me!

The following workouts allow you to focus on each form of point of view—first, second and third.

And remember, in each form, you and the book narrator are one.

To discover your point of view, take the same steps as you did when working with tone:

- Connect to the story.
- Identify the point of view you are reading with.
- Apply that point of view the next time you read the story.

Here's a reminder of the techniques and tools you can use to achieve the above.

```
Read Out loud
    Slow it Down
        Do Nothing
            Note it
                Welcome the Unexpected
                    Don't Overdo it
                        Read as if to Someone You Know
```

First Person: Fiction

The first-person book narrator is almost always the main character and, unless that book narrator is a psychic or a ghost, he or she cannot be sure what is in the other characters' minds. The first-person book narrator tells the story only from their point of view; how they see the events and characters.

First Person: Fiction Workouts

Find your point of view in this story.

Text: THE TRIP

I couldn't believe our luck. We'd slogged through thirty miles of muddy red earth for over five hours in a barely held together minibus, the pride of the local population. We were averaging an 'amazing' six miles an hour and shared the ride with two women carrying a goat that was baaing loudly, one woman carrying a baby that soon started wailing, and an old man who scolded the driver any time the bus slowed down. And to top all of that, Armand and I had to get out and help dig the minibus out of a rut the size of Texas. Twice.

Did you—and thus the book narrator—see this as a great experience? Maybe the point of view you gave her was *this is a fabulous adventure,* and the tone was *gung-ho* or *zesty* or *feisty* or *eager.* Her personality in that case might be fun loving or open and curious.

Following is the text with examples of notes reflecting a *this is a fabulous adventure* point of view.

Text: THE TRIP (with notes)

I couldn't believe our luck. We'd slogged through thirty miles of muddy red earth for over five hours *HA* in a barely held together minibus, the pride of the local population. We were averaging an 'amazing' six miles an hour and shared the ride with two women carrying a goat that was baaing loudly, *LOVE IT* one woman carrying a baby *AWWW* that soon started wailing, and an old man who scolded the driver any time the bus slowed down. And to top all of that, *GET THIS* Armand and I had to get out and help dig the minibus out of a rut the size of Texas. *FUN* Twice.

Perhaps as you worked, you saw the situation differently, as no fun at all. Maybe your point of view was *this is a nightmare,* and the tone was *disdainful,* or *indignant, annoyed* or *scornful.* In that case, your book narrator might have a pessimistic personality, is snarky and finds fault with everything. The point of view you use reflects the book narrator's personality. An open, curious, fun-loving person will see things quite differently than a snarky, disdainful one.

Read the selection again, but this time take the opposite point of view from the one you originally came up with. Think of it as a defined point of view and work with it the same way you worked with a defined tone. Keep that point of view in mind and see where it takes you.

Following is the text with examples of notes reflecting a *cynical* point of view.

Text: THE TRIP (with notes)

I couldn't believe our luck. We'd slogged *AGONY* through thirty miles of muddy *ANNOYED* red earth for over five *GRUELING* hours in a *EMPHASIZE* barely held together minibus, the pride of the local population. We were averaging an 'amazing' *SARCASTIC* six miles an hour and shared the ride with two women carrying a goat *EEW* that was baaing loudly, one woman carrying a baby that soon started wailing, *DISMAY* and an old man who scolded the driver any time the bus slowed down. And to top all of that, *IRRITATED* Armand and I had to get out and help dig the minibus out of a rut the size of Texas. *WHY DID I DO THIS* Twice.

Let's expand THE TRIP to include additional text that presents Armand's reactions. Use the defined point of view that *the trip was a fabulous adventure.*

Remember, the first-person book narrator can only see the story from his or her point of view. Armand may see things from a negative, grouchy point of view, but you don't convey Armand's reaction from his point of view, you convey it from the book narrator's.

Text: THE TRIP (expanded)

I couldn't believe our luck. We'd slogged through thirty miles of muddy red earth for over five hours in a barely held together minibus, the pride of the local population. We were averaging an 'amazing' six miles an hour and shared the ride with two women carrying a goat that was baaing loudly, one woman carrying a baby that soon started wailing, and an old man who scolded the driver any time the bus slowed down. And to top all of that, Armand and I had to get out and help dig the minibus out of a rut the size of Texas. Twice.

We had pretty much run out of water, just a few drops left per our two bottles, and Armand, crabby as ever, kept complaining that the heat was sucking the juice out of him. He is usually a guy who sees the glass as half empty. This time he was seeing it as totally empty. He was getting to be a downer.

Okay, even I wasn't sure our water would last long enough to get us into the village where we could hopefully buy a couple of bottles of water. Or at least soda. Every store sells some kind of soda.

Oh, and about the luck part? It's that we made it. We didn't drop of heat exhaustion or dehydration.

We'd been planning to stay in this village for about a week, find our long-lost buddy D'Arcy, chill for a bit and then find another way back to the town.

Let's expand THE TRIP again. In every book, new events and characters appear, and as you read, the point of view you originally used may seem like it should change. That may turn out to be true, but even if events in the story are not what you expected, don't rush to change your point of view until you are sure the one you're working with is definitely not right for the material. Sticking to it can give you a very interesting reading. See what happens when you allow yourself to explore an unexpected twist and you Welcome the Unexpected.

In this further expansion of THE TRIP, the situation becomes threatening. Begin with the defined point of view: *this was a fabulous adventure*. A person who sees the events as a great adventure could easily keep her upbeat approach when telling the story of being in danger.

Text: THE TRIP (further expanded)

I couldn't believe our luck. We'd slogged through thirty miles of muddy red earth for over five hours in a barely held together minibus, the pride of the local population. We were averaging an 'amazing' six miles an hour and shared the ride with two women carrying a goat that was baaing loudly, one woman carrying a baby that soon started wailing, and an old man who scolded the driver any time the bus slowed down. And to top all of that, Armand and I had to get out and help dig the minibus out of a rut the size of Texas. Twice.

We had pretty much run out of water, just a few drops left per our two bottles, and Armand, crabby as ever, kept complaining that the heat was sucking the juice out of him. He is usually a guy who sees the glass as half empty. This time he was seeing it as totally empty. He was getting to be a downer.

Okay, even I wasn't sure our water would last long enough to get us into the village where we could hopefully buy a couple of bottles of water. Or at least soda. Every store sells some kind of soda.

Oh, and about the luck part? It's that we made it. We didn't drop of heat exhaustion or dehydration.

We'd been planning to stay in this village for about a week, find our long-lost buddy D'Arcy, chill for a bit and then find another way back to the town. But I immediately knew I'd have to stay here longer, get a feel of the place, and its wonderful assortment of people. Armand, though, decided to move on.

I'd taken a room in a little guest house. I'd been there a week when one night, at about 11 p.m., I left for dinner and was set on by three men and forced back to my room. They stole nearly everything. Money? Gone! Bags? Gone! Watch? Gone! Luckily, they let me keep the clothes I was wearing. Also luckily, the bus driver that stopped at the village the next day agreed to haul me back to civilization, but at an increased price, adding a bit of interest, for his having trusted that I'd pay when we made it back to town.

How did you react? Were you able to maintain your *this is a fabulous adventure* point of view? Did you find the new situation kind of funny and were you able to tell the story as if it was part of the great adventure? Or did the new material change how you felt about the story? Did it make you see things from a different point of view? Maybe now your book narrator was someone who saw things negatively and you want to change the point of view to *this was a big mistake!* That would be fine. If it happens, give it a try. As a story progresses, you might find that new details guide you in a different direction.

In this next selection, you get a chance to be a criminal. See how it feels to be really bad.

Text: EASY MONEY

It was three AM, and the town was shutting down. I wasn't expecting anything to happen, but this guy suddenly appeared. He was neat, clean, wearing a good-looking suit. Yeah, I know a good suit, and I knew that suit meant money. Easy money.

I don't like a fuss. I don't want to have to use a knife or a gun on anyone. I prefer things simple, like this was. That doesn't mean it didn't excite me. Seeing a mark like this made my day real special. I was in his face for a second and then he was practically begging me to take his wallet, like he was giving me a Christmas present, but just forgot the wrapping.

It's pretty easy to see this book narrator as a tough, no-holds barred sociopath whose point of view is that *life is one big smackdown.* With that point of view, the resulting tone might be *tough*, or *hard edged.* But as you read, did other reactions emerge? For example, maybe you saw this book narrator as a thief with a dramatic flair, someone who loved to show off. In that case your point of view might become *suckers get what they deserve.*

Or what if, instead, you found the events humorous as you read, and in your hands, the book narrator was a cool, slick character who saw the events as funny and of no consequence, like one of those thieves we've seen in a movie—the glamorous, seductive, amoral charmer. Your point of view might become *life is just a game to be played.*

Let's expand the selection. In this version the book narrator describes his victim's reaction. Use the point of view and tone you came up with for this story and remember, the first-person book narrator sees things only from his point of view. You convey how he/you see the events, not how the victim does.

Text: EASY MONEY (expanded)

It was 3 a.m., and the town was shutting down. I wasn't expecting anything to happen, but this guy suddenly appeared. He was neat, clean, wearing a good-looking suit. Yeah, I know a good suit, and I knew that suit meant money. Easy money.

I don't like a fuss. I don't want to have to use a knife or a gun on anyone. I prefer things simple, like this was. That doesn't mean it didn't excite me. Seeing a mark like this made my day real special. I was in his face for a second and then he was practically begging me to take his wallet, like he was giving me a Christmas present, but just forgot the wrapping. He was shaking like a pair of maracas in some Mexican band. Sweat was pourin' down his face and I swear his eyes were bugging way outta their sockets.

From the victim's point of view, the situation may be terrifying and he's likely hoping for mercy, but from the from the book narrator's point of view, the victim's fear may be worthy of his scorn or mockery or laughter.

First Person: Nonfiction

Memoirs, autobiographies, recounting of personal adventures, stories about how someone approached their scientific research or, as in the following—an author's experience creating an exercise program geared to a particular population—are all true stories told in first person. Publishers generally prefer that authors read their own first-person nonfiction books because it adds authenticity to the listening experience. Many years ago I worked with the late Senator John McCain on several of his audiobook recordings including *Faith of My Fathers*. His life story—the torture he withstood while imprisoned during the Vietnam War, the sacrifices he made and the values he held—was best told by him.

Still, an author may be unavailable or reluctant to read their work. In that case, the job will go to an actor who can reasonably represent the author's sound, style, and point of view. You don't have to be an impersonator, but you do have to be in the ballpark of the author's approach.

You want to convey the author's manner of speech: does he speak gently, is he precise, does he have an interesting rhythm pattern? Identifying those aspects of speech are covered fully in chapter ten, Character Voices for Adults. To help you identify the author's sound and speech pattern, you can refer to samples of their interviews or speeches. They're easy to find, especially if the author is well known.

Once you're familiar with the author's sound, choose a point of view consistent with his or her style. For example, does she take a hard line on issues, indicating that her point of view is *I brook no opposition*? Or does she sound compassionate, indicating that her point of view is *I want you to be comfortable with this material*? Does she use humor, indicating her point of view might be *don't take things too seriously?* Knowing the author's style and point of view is a lot like a publisher defining the book's tone. So choose the point of view best suited for that person and begin from there.

Of course you may be asked to read a book by an author for whom there are no voice references. Or the material, while extremely important, wasn't written by a well-known figure, so capturing their sound isn't critical. It's the point of view and the tone of the book you want to convey.

First Person: Nonfiction Workout

What point of view do you come up with for the developer of this training system? Do you see it from the point of view of someone giving authoritative information or as someone providing encouragement? Or perhaps you see it from the point of view of conveying compassion and reassurance about people's issues about aging.

Text: FOCUSED, PROGRESSIVE TRAINING

I've spent my whole training career keeping seniors fit, active and independent. Most of my clients began training with me because they noticed that getting out of a chair or picking things up from the floor was a lot harder and slower than it used to be. And getting up from the floor without something to hold on to had become unthinkable.

One sixty-eight-year-old client came to me because he couldn't get up from the blanket he was lying on in the park and had to be hoisted up by two burly teenagers. He was shocked, embarrassed and worst of all, he felt helpless to change his situation. He thought he'd reached a stage from which there was no return, believing he was experiencing 'the unavoidable decline' that happens when you grow old: you get stiff and slow, your strength fades, and your balance gets sketchy.

That's what most people believe.

But that belief is false! You have a choice. Those changes are not inevitable. You can choose to retain the functionality that you have, improve it or even regain lost function. You can increase your strength and muscle mass at any age, and your mind does not have to slow down as you get older.

I'm not naive. I know what we're up against. We've all seen the talk shows and newspaper articles with experts pointing to charts and graphs. We've heard them tell us that our mind, muscle, and functionality will decrease at a predictable rate. They'd have us believe that planning for our golden years involves knee and hip replacements, substituting ramps for stairs, and the researching of nursing homes.

They have promoted a concept, the concept of inevitability. I know they are well meaning, but they have it wrong.

I know they're wrong because my clients and I have been proving them wrong for years. None of those negative changes associated with age are inevitable. All you need is a plan to avoid those negative changes and the will to see it through. And what you hold in your hands is that plan.

It's called Focused, Progressive Training.

This training program incorporates powerful techniques and approaches gathered during my years as a ballet dancer trained in the Ballet Rousse style, an amateur boxer, a hard-style kettlebell instructor and a Muscle Activation Technique specialist. And though these seem to be unrelated disciplines, they all have a common thread: the emphasis of strength and flexibility through efficiency. That is what you'll gain by following this program.[1]

Whatever point of view you chose in the previous three selections, the first-person book narrators were describing events realistically. Their facts are correct. They are *reliable* narrators. Not every first-person book narrator, however, is quite so reliable.

---

[1] Text FOCUSED, PROGRESSIVE TRAINING by Neil Mitchell.

First Person: The Unreliable Book Narrator

This type of book narrator is not providing accurate information about the events or facts in a story. He may be purposely distorting or misrepresenting them, or he may have an inaccurate vision of reality. Whatever the reason, remember: you and the book narrator are one. You aren't mocking this book narrator; you are not trying to signal his distortions or misconceptions. The listener will get that from the dissonance between his point of view and the truth as it becomes apparent in the story.

First Person: The Unreliable Book Narrator Workout

The Tell-Tale Heart, by Edgar Allan Poe, presents a wonderfully unreliable narrator. His point of view as to why he killed the old man with whom he lived is totally at odds with reality. For example, this book narrator explains that it was the dead man's eye that drove him to commit the murder. He hated the old man's cloudy blue eye; it was a "vulture eye," an evil eye. He believes that's a totally reasonable explanation, which it might be for a totally delusional person.

The character's insanity reveals itself soon enough but not because you signal it or take a judgmental attitude toward him. You are conveying how he sees things. He provides a torrent of information that he believes demonstrates his rationality, but of course, what he says just confirms his madness and thus his unreliability.

Remember, you and this book narrator are one for the duration of the story. Don't approach it from a predetermined idea of how a madman would see things. Find the madman lurking within you.

Text: *THE TELL-TALE HEART* (excerpt)

TRUE!—nervous—very, very dreadfully nervous I had been and am; but why will you say that I am mad? The disease had sharpened my senses—not destroyed—not dulled them.

Above all was the sense of hearing acute. I heard all things in the heaven and in the earth. I heard many things in hell. How, then, am I mad? Hearken! And observe how healthily—how calmly I can tell you the whole story.

It is impossible to say how first the idea entered my brain; but once conceived, it haunted me day and night. Object there was none. Passion there was none. I loved the old man. He had never wronged me. He had never given me insult. For his gold I had no desire. I think it was his eye!

Yes, it was this! He had the eye of a vulture—a pale blue eye, with a film over it. Whenever it fell upon me, my blood ran cold; and so by degrees—very gradually—I made up my mind to take the life of the old man, and thus rid myself of the eye forever.

Now this is the point. You fancy me mad. Madmen know nothing. But you should have seen me. You should have seen how wisely I proceeded—with what caution—with what foresight—with what dissimulation I went to work!

I was never kinder to the old man than during the whole week before I killed him. And every night, about midnight, I turned the latch of his door and opened it—oh so gently! And then, when I had made an opening sufficient for my head, I put in a dark lantern, all closed, closed, so that no light shone out, and then I thrust in my head.

Oh, you would have laughed to see how cunningly I thrust it in! I moved it slowly—very, very slowly, so that I might not disturb the old man's sleep. It took me an hour to place my whole head within the opening so far that I could see him as he lay upon his bed.

Ha!—would a madman have been so wise as this?

If you haven't come up with a point of view you're satisfied with, try one of the following:

Possible Point of View: *The murder was totally justifiable.*
Possible Personality: *Paranoid.*
Possible Tone: *Reasonable.*

Alternate Point of View: *Everyone must be challenged.*
Alternate Personality: *Manic.*
Alternate Tone: *Aggressive.*

The first-person book narrator in Poe's short story *The Tell-Tale Heart* is the main character. Most first-person book narrators are. You may, however, encounter some who are not.

First Person: Who is not the Main Character

In this perspective, the book narrator tells a story focused on someone else who is the main character. This book narrator may be a participant in the story or may be telling a story about events in which they didn't participate. Since it's told in first person, this book narrator also can only see things from their own point of view, not that of the main character.

First Person: Who Is Not The Main Character Workout

In the following selection, the first-person book narrator, the one telling the story, is not the main character. Peter is. He drives the events. He may be excited by what is happening and likely sees it as a fantastic experience. But do you, and thus the book narrator, see things that way? Or do you have a different point of view about the experience?

Text: PETER'S STORY

It was Thursday and a small group of us were lolling around Peter's house. Peter was a writer who loved a challenge and that day he'd been galvanized by what he saw as his greatest, most monumental challenge ever.

He'd been reading a book about black magic when he suddenly announced, "This coming Sunday is one of the most magical and powerful of days. On this day there will be a truly rare confluence of stars and cosmic influences. On this day," he paused for effect then lowered his voice to a confidential whisper, "the devil himself can be called forth and battled!"

Peter looked up, his coal-black eyes glittering. "Do you realize that we will be able to do the unthinkable? We will be able to challenge the devil."

Okay, I knew that Peter was a little crazy. But his was usually a good kind of crazy, a wildly imaginative crazy that made things brighter, sharper. He could tease out an unexpected adventurousness in us, burrow into our secret places and awaken a different kind of engagement with the world; one that was kaleidoscopic, colorful and daring. And that was really what we were all looking for—an access route to our own rebelliousness and off-the-wall creativity.

His house was central headquarters for up-and-coming musicians, comics, artists, writers and one hooker. It was also smack in the middle of a conservative section of Greenwich Village, where the aging mothers of some major mobsters lived.

"Maybe this is not the ideal location for a Black Sabbath devil-call-out," I offered. "I mean, according to the instructions, we'll have to set up a gallows and a hangman's noose."

But Peter was adamant. The whole thing would be fun, a once in a lifetime experience to call down the devil. All we needed, he insisted, were a few more people, well twelve in total, an oil lamp, oil, and the proper effigy to hang from the noose and the gallows. No big deal.

In the face of our reluctance, he was relentless. He pressed on and on, swatting away our detailed objections like some annoying no-see-ums until somehow, we all began to recognize the same miraculous possibilities he did. His manic energy, the fact that it was the '60s, and the idea that we each would play a unique role in this most extraordinary of planetary healing rituals was too much to resist. After all, who wouldn't want to elevate the consciousness of the world and face down the devil if given the chance?

So, we went to work. We easily found nine other participants. It turned out that there were a whole lot of people in those days eager to participate in a ritual…any kind of ritual.

We scrounged up some wood and set up a gallows and noose in front of the floor-to-ceiling sliding glass doors that faced a courtyard surrounded by buildings occupied by many of the mob mothers. A deeply religious group, I suspected they would not take kindly to the noose, not to mention the accompanying chanting and possibly terrified screaming we'd be doing were the horned one to actually appear. The thought did occur to me that perhaps, just perhaps, Peter himself was the devil. But that was only many years later.

Possible Point of View: *This was such a hoot.*
Possible Personality: *Warm, funny.*
Possible Tone: *Spunky, effervescent.*

Alternate Point of View: *What a waste of time! What were we thinking?*
Alternate Personality: *Tough, sarcastic.*
Alternate Tone: *Ironic.*

Once you've come up with the point of view and tone, try out one noted above. If you initially used one of the above suggestions, try the other one. The more flexible you are, the easier it will be to adjust when a publisher or writer asks for a particular point of view or tone that leads you in a direction you hadn't anticipated.

Second Person: Fiction

Here the book narrator tells a story to, and about, an unidentified 'you.' This book narrator seems to know everything about what that 'you' is doing, feeling and thinking.

In this form, one of the possibilities is that the 'you' in the story is an unseen listener. Read the following text as if the 'you' is that unseen listener the book narrator is addressing.

Second Person: Fiction Workout

Text: THE KITCHEN

You step into the kitchen. Dishes are stacked in the sink. You are angry, remembering last night, and that hot stone living in your chest presses down hard. You reach for a dish and then smash it to the floor. You're not proud of yourself, not for last night and not for the dish. Light pours through the window and you yank the curtain down hard. Do you think that will protect you?

Another interesting possibility in second person fiction is that the book narrator is actually the 'you' in the story. In other words, the book narrator is addressing herself. She is both speaker and the one being spoken to. Read THE KITCHEN text again, but this time, make the 'you,' you. Take a breath and go for it. Talk to yourself! We've all done it, although maybe not in public.

Text: THE KITCHEN

You step into the kitchen. Dishes are stacked in the sink. You are angry, remembering last night, and that hot stone living in your chest presses down hard. You reach for a dish and then smash it to the floor. You're not proud of yourself, not for last night and not for the dish. Light pours through the window and you yank the curtain down hard. Do you think that will protect you?

How did you react to addressing the two different 'yous?' Did you give each version a different point of view and tone? Did each version give rise to very different emotions or were your responses similar?

The following excerpt from Nathaniel Hawthorne's *The Haunted Mind*, (in *Twice Told Tales)*, is written in second person. The descriptive immediacy and specificity of the language strongly indicates that the book narrator is also the 'you' in the story. But, perhaps in your reading, you'll be speaking to an unseen listener.

Text: THE HAUNTED MIND (excerpt)

What a singular moment is the first one, when you have hardly begun to recollect yourself after starting from midnight slumber! By unclosing your eyes so suddenly, you seem to have surprised the personages of your dream in full convocation round your bed, and catch one broad glance at them before they can flit into obscurity. Or, to vary the metaphor, you find yourself, for a single instant, wide awake in that realm of illusions, whither sleep has been the passport, and behold its ghostly inhabitants and wondrous scenery, with a perception of their strangeness, such as you never attain while the dream is undisturbed.

What did the story evoke in you?: Who was the you? Yourself or someone else? What point of view did you come up with? What tone did it give rise to? Even though second-person fiction is a form not often used, it's interesting and so is very worth exploring.

Second Person: Nonfiction

Second person is frequently used for nonfiction, especially for instructional and self-help books. The form allows the author, and you, the audiobook actor, to speak very directly and personally to the listener.

I directed a doctor's reading of his book about preventing and curing illness with food. It was a dry, straightforward instructional book, written in second person. Listening to the good doctor describe medical conditions and the foods you should eat for your health was—to be kind—coma inducing. If I was in danger of becoming unconscious, I could only imagine listeners' responses.

And some of them might be driving.

An intervention was required.

I asked the doctor why he'd written the book. He explained how important it was to him that people understood the power of food to help them fight their medical problems. That helped clarify his point of view: *People can help themselves with this information.* But the doctor wasn't reading the book with that in mind. He was just reciting facts and his recommendations.

After a bit of discussion and a few short in-studio rehearsals, he was able to infuse his reading with his point of view, that of a doctor who wanted to *inspire patients with knowledge*. With that point of view, the tone became *caring*. The personality of the book narrator/doctor went from *boring* to *wise*.

The doctor's reading didn't suddenly become amazing, but he was no longer in danger of putting anyone to sleep or causing a traffic accident.

If the author of this form of book is well known, you can approach it as you do with first-person nonfiction: choose a point of view consistent with the author's approach. For example, he sees things from a humorous point of view, or she connects to her audience with deep sincerity, or she conveys her sense of urgency about her topic. Think of it as a given point of view and begin reading with that point of view in mind. If the author is not well known, discover the point of view that will make the material interesting and keep the listener wanting to learn more.

Second Person: Nonfiction Workout

Let's return to FOCUSED, PROGRESSIVE TRAINING. While the introduction is written in first person, the rest of this instructional is written in second person. In this section, the author is talking directly to the reader, providing critical information and things to do prior to beginning the exercise program. Read as if communicating with your unseen listener. The technique of 'Read as if to Someone You Know' might be helpful here. When you've finished the reading, identify the point of view and tone that you were using.

Text: FOCUSED, PROGRESSIVE TRAINING

Your doctor's approval is of vital importance for your health and safety. Those of you who are either new to exercising or who have been leading a sedentary lifestyle may have physical problems you are unaware of, simply because you've never exerted yourself to the point of showing symptoms.

If you start *any* training or exercise program without getting checked out medically, those problems may be exposed quickly and painfully. Get your doctor's okay before starting this or any new program.

KNOW WHEN TO SAY NO

Always be realistic about your physical condition and present capabilities. Do as many of the movements and exercises as you are capable of doing, but if there are some you can't do, it's okay. There's no need to lose your enthusiasm or drive because you can't do everything.

Your goal is not to do exercises; your goal is to make your body stronger and more functional than it is now. Many of my clients have made life-altering changes by mastering just a few of the exercises and concepts in this manual.

So, if you can't do everything right away, or if you have to skip some exercises entirely, don't be concerned. Just go as far as you can and do as many of the exercises as your body (and your doctor) will allow. This will give you a training program customized to your personal physical capabilities. Mastering the simplest techniques of just a few exercises will yield powerful results.

<u>Use Common Sense</u>

• If you're sick, don't work out.

• If your doctor tells you not to do something, don't do it.

• If an activity or movement causes pain in one or more of your joints, stop doing that movement and get the problem checked out.

• Be aware of your environment. If, for example, there are low ceilings or trip hazards, a slippery floor or over-crowded conditions, correct the ones that are in your control or find another space where it's safe to train.

No set of rules can cover every possible circumstance. Always use common sense and never put yourself in dangerous situations.[1]

Third Person: Fiction

The third-person book narrator tells a story in which he or she is not a participant and does not refer to him or herself in the book. This book narrator, however, knows all the details of the story they are telling, and what all the characters are feeling and experiencing. Too often, actors think that reading in third person means you have to emotionally stay out of the story and just report it, like our aforementioned 'no point of view, no tone' actor. By now, you've experienced how powerful using point of view and tone are for first and second-person book narrators. It works the same way for the third-person book narrator. By giving

---

[1] Text Focused, Progressive Training by Neil Mitchell.

him or her a point of view, and responding to the story, you create a performance rather than a rote recitation.

Third Person: Fiction Workouts

The following is an excerpt from the book, *What Maisie Knew* by Henry James. The point of view you come up with here doesn't have to be what you'd come up with after reading the entire novel. Approach it as a stand-alone piece. Assume the book narrator is talking about events he's witnessed and people he knows and understands.

Remember:

Read Out Loud
　　Slow it Down
　　　　Do Nothing
　　　　　　Note it
　　　　　　　　Welcome the Unexpected
　　　　　　　　　　Don't Overdo it
　　　　　　　　　　　　Read as if to Someone You Know

Text: *WHAT MAISIE KNEW* (excerpt)

The litigation had seemed interminable and had in fact been complicated; but by the decision on the appeal the judgment of the divorce-court was confirmed as to the assignment of the child. The father, who, though bespattered from head to foot, had made good his case, was, in pursuance of this triumph, appointed to keep her: it was not so much that the mother's character had been more absolutely damaged as that the brilliancy of a lady's complexion (and this lady's, in court, was immensely remarked) might be more regarded as showing the spots. Attached, however, to the second pronouncement was a condition that detracted, for Beale Farange, from its sweetness—an order that he should refund to his late wife the twenty-six hundred pounds put down by her, as it was called, some three years before, in the interest of the child's maintenance and precisely on a proved understanding that he would take no proceedings: a sum of which he had had the administration, and of which he could render not the least account. The obligation thus attributed to her adversary was no small balm to Ida's resentment; it drew a part of the sting from her defeat and compelled Mr. Farange perceptibly to lower his crest. He was unable to produce the money or to raise it in any way; so that after a squabble scarcely less public and scarcely more decent than the original shock of battle his only issue from his predicament was a compromise proposed by his legal advisers and finally accepted by hers.

His debt was by this arrangement remitted to him and the little girl disposed of in a manner worthy of the judgement-seat of Solomon. She was divided in two and the portions tossed impartially to the disputants. They would take her, in rotation, for six months at a time; she would spend half the year with each. This was odd justice in the eyes of those who still blinked in the fierce light projected from the tribunal—a light in which neither parent figured in the least as a happy example to youth and innocence. What was to have been expected on the evidence was the nomination, in loco parentis, of some proper third person, some respectable or at least some presentable friend. Apparently, however, the circle of the Faranges had been scanned in vain for any such ornament; so that the only solution finally meeting all the difficulties was, save that of sending Maisie to a Home, the partition of the tutelary office in the manner I have mentioned. There were more reasons for her parents to agree to it than there had ever been for them to agree to anything; and they now prepared with her help to enjoy the distinction that waits upon vulgarity sufficiently attested.

How did you see things? Was your point of view that the *litigants and proceedings deserved disdain*, thus giving the book narrator a smug, condemnatory personality? Or did you create a more caring person from whose point of view *the people deserved sympathy* and the situation deserved the utmost of *respect*? Then again, maybe your book narrator saw the situation as a *hilarious circus*.

Any of these choices would give you a very unique and interesting read.

In this next selection, Mary, an older detective, is giving up her traditional way of doing things and is facing the unfamiliar world of tech.

Text: MARY

Mary looked at the computer on her desk. It had taken her a while to get used to it. Of course she liked the ease of searches and of accessing data bases, at least she was trying to learn and get up to speed on it. But she'd been typing up forms for so long and writing memos, mostly to herself, it felt as if her typewriter was her friend. She knew the feel of its keys and the sound it made with each finger strike. And, as is often the case with people and their machines, she secretly thought it knew her touch and responded to her. Of course it wasn't actually her typewriter, it belonged to the department. Still, it felt like hers. She understood that thinking a typewriter would know her was unrealistic. But she was, in her way, a dreamer. She'd always wanted to be a cop, so if she had been realistic she might never have joined the force. She would have been realistic about how hard she'd have to fight to prove herself. She'd have been realistic about the toll it would take until another woman joined and then another and another until suddenly, she wasn't alone. It wasn't just Mary staunchly facing the pranks, the snide digs and the constant testing by her reluctant partner. It had taken time to change the culture of resentment to one of respect. Maybe that's why she liked her typewriter, it never made her feel unwanted. It was right there, trusting and ready to get down to work with her. She was hoping her computer would be ready to do the same.

Possible Point of View: *Change is hard.*
Possible Tone: *Sympathetic.*

Alternate Point of View: *This woman is one tough gal.*
Alternate Tone: *Sassy.*

In the following selection, the third person book narrator tells a story about two characters whose responses to the situation they're in are quite different. Find your point of view, the tone of the story, and see how you can convey what both characters are feeling.

Text: THE HIKE

The sun was barely visible now. There was little chance they'd be able to find their way down once it had finally set. Danny looked down the mountain. It was steep and intimidating. The rocky outcroppings seemed foreboding and the shadows now falling across the landscape made it even harder to find a safe path out. Danny moved very slowly, knowing that the smallest false step would put him in terrible danger. Suddenly, several rocks came loose just above his position. They were tumbling now, falling in front of him and he stopped. He reached his hand out, feeling for a something solid to grasp, some secured rock that he could hold fast to, and over which he could exert a semblance of control, even though it was, he knew, a mere illusion of control. Still, it was all he had.

Just behind him, Angela was preparing for nightfall; but instead of fearing it, she was yielding to the night's promise. She silently looked up into what seemed almost an invitation to the darkness, to the mystery she sensed everywhere. She held herself against the incline and against the night, as if in a lover's embrace. She would trust the dark and this mountain that Danny now deeply feared.

Possible Point of View: *This is an extraordinary night.*
Possible Tone: *Fervent, heart-pounding, raw.*

Third Person: Nonfiction

In third person nonfiction, the book narrator is expressing the author's point of view. That would be like having a defined point of view for the material. If the writer is well known, you'll want capture their flavor, their emotional approach when speaking on their topic. You can find that by listening to interviews or lectures they've given that can be accessed online. If the author is not well known, you have the freedom to dig in and discover what point of view to give the material that makes it more than just information.

Third Person: Nonfiction Workout

In the following essay, the topic is the idea of 'othering.' The story is about how we humans organize ourselves and the results of that organization. The author is unknown, and the material could easily be seen as merely instructive. But what happens when you move past the surface of the material? What happens when you discover an engaging point of view?

Text: OTHERING

Every culture establishes a set of normative values, interpersonal relationships, spiritual meaning, and even what foods are considered tasty—from insects to jellied blood, from camel tendons to mashed potatoes and peas. Cultural values, food preferences, clothing styles, are some of the things that bond a society. Those who are outside the group, those who don't share its values, are often suspect, disdained.

Human life itself is dependent on culture, the shared information, values and regulations that provide a framework in which members of that culture operate, develop and create.

There is, however, a negative side to the power of a shared culture: the dehumanizing of those not in the group, the seeing of them as the 'other,' as brutes, an infestation, subhuman. 'Othering' is found everywhere and it has led to extraordinary cruelty; cruelty to an extent unknown in other species.

It was the work of anthropologists that led to a realization that what is thought to be normal, is actually relative: that one group's truths are not the only truths, and that human beings have a tremendous capacity to create and internalize an incredibly diverse set of beliefs, values, tastes and organizational principals. And it is the work of anthropologists, as well as that of historians, philosophers, psychologists, et al, that presents us with the possibility of recognizing our core commonality and seeing everyone as 'us.'

Possible Point of View: *I can inspire change.*
Possible Tone: *Uplifting.*
Possible Personality: *Caring.*

Alternate Point of View: *This is critical knowledge.*
Alternate Tone: *Committed.*
Alternate Personality: *Intense.*

As you work, the author's story—the events, the characters, language, imagery and culture in which the story takes place—fuels your imagination. When you allow yourself the freedom to explore, you will find nuances, ideas and creative responses to the book that are unique to you, and thus, you are finding your truth within the author's, making it your story too.

PART THREE

FINDING YOUR TRUTH WITHIN THE AUTHOR'S

There's something special about hearing my words in someone else's voice. It's a feeling that the text isn't just mine anymore, that there's a certain amount of ownership of the text by the world and by other people who are producing it and listening to it and giving voice to it and bringing it alive.

—David Anthony Durham[1]

[1] David Anthony Durham, "Talking with David Anthony Durham," *AudoFile* magazine, February/March, 2010.

5

The Language Style

If you wish to know the mind of a man, listen to his words.
—Johann Wolfgang von Goethe

The author's language style—their choice of words, the complexity or brevity of their sentences, the rhythm of those sentences, the delicacy or toughness of their wording, the compactness, the use of poetic imagery, the lack of it, the terseness, the gentle flow—are all tools by which the author shapes the story.

While a book's words do not dictate a tone or a point of view, the language style, the way the author uses words, will affect how you respond to that story. You wouldn't respond to a hard-hitting no-waste-of-words book by Hemingway as you would to an ethereal, romantic novel. You might give a detective story a *sardonic* tone, or a *flip* tone, or a *hard-boiled* tone, but you wouldn't respond to it as if it were a *flighty* comedy. Nor would you give a light-hearted romantic story a *tough* or *aggressive* tone.

The emotionally responsive work you do on tone and point of view enables you to work with the author's language style and discover an essence, an interpretation that no other actor will, though you are each responding to the same language style and story.

Language Style Workouts

In the story HONDURAS (which is based on actual events), you'll work with a style that is compact and muscular. The author's language is active and specific. The story is about people in a dangerous, perhaps terrifying situation. The first-person book narrator has flown into Honduras, pre-9/11, with his girlfriend, Sofia, and his handgun. Though he followed pre-9/11 international protocol, the gun was confiscated at baggage, and he and Sofia have been taken into custody by the Honduran police.

As you read, remember that you and the book narrator are one. What he feels and sees, you feel and see. Your point of view is his. Though it's doubtful you've been in the author's situation, you've likely been in a dangerous or nerve-wracking predicament. And if not, you know what it feels like to be tense or frightened. Be aware of how the author's vocabulary and his sentence style make you feel that tension, how the language guides you and helps you discover your point of view and tone. Though a man would be chosen to read HONDURAS, don't limit yourself. Everyone should read it and give it their own interpretation.

Text: HONDURAS

We were surrounded by military police and escorted out of the airport to a waiting sedan. One of the policemen sat in front and we two were placed in the back. Sofia inquired in Spanish as to our destination but was met with silence bordering on disdain. That, combined with the lack of air-conditioning in the car, brought us to a higher level of concern and perspiration.

The car followed the pothole-scarred airport highway for about a half-hour before turning off at the older part of the capital city. The poverty, unseen by visitors flying in, was in full array all around us: toothless old ladies working the streets, younger ones like beasts of burden carrying all manner of things: bundles of old clothes wrapped in twine, buckets of unspeakable liquids. Sewage and garbage were strewn everywhere. We quickly turned a corner and were presented with a most ominous sight, a combination police station and what I assumed to be a jailhouse but was in fact one of the huge federal prisons, a monolithic, yellowing ugly concrete structure forty feet high and topped by watch towers at the corners and razor wire in between. The situation was getting increasingly dire by the moment.

The car circled to the entrance of the prison, an enormous medieval-looking iron gate manned by two sentries in combat uniforms. The driver stopped, leaned out the window and mumbled something to one of them in colloquial Spanish that I didn't understand. The gate, with a loud clanking noise, began to rise slowly. We were directed to a parking area. The car stopped. The officer in front opened the door for us and we emerged sweaty and concerned and were led to a stone archway, the door to the building. Dim hallway lights reflected off of the granite bricks of the ancient construction, foreboding and evil.

A couple of turns and we came to the office of the Comandante, the boss. We entered and were ushered into the big man's inner sanctum, an institutional looking gray room with a gray chair, gray file cabinets and a very gray Comandante who was seated at a steel desk, also gray.

General Perez couldn't have been more than five foot one, a dead ringer for Danny DeVito, with very greasy hair. On the desk, in full view, was my .45.[1]

The language style in HONDURAS wastes no time, the sentences don't muse and meander; they are forceful and get to the point. The imagery, combined with the situation, leaves no room for doubt that

[1] Text Honduras by Ira Marks.

these characters are in danger. The author increases the tension with his descriptions of the streets and of the prison: medieval, monolithic with granite bricks, a yellow, ugly concrete structure.

One actor's point of view when reading the story was *must stay on high alert*. He saw the book narrator as someone with a tough personality, a gun user and a man who was extremely observant and aware of everything around him. The tone he gave the story was *extreme tension*. But another actor responded differently. He felt the use of the word 'concern' twice, instead of a more powerful word like 'fear,' indicated that the book narrator was in denial, protecting himself against what was facing him. His point of view was *keep it steady*. He saw the man as frightened, but able to create a false sense of reality. The tone he used was *defensive*. Both interpretations honored the story, the language and style of the text while providing unique performances.

In contrast to HONDURAS, the following selection uses a delicate vocabulary with language that evokes light and air. Find your point of view and tone consistent with the story and the delicacy of the author's language.

Text: CHIARASCURO

The light drifted slowly across the room, falling gracefully on the delicate patterns of the softly colored rug. The chiaroscuro resonances were like music, delicate tones shifting as the curtains responded to the warm, island breeze. Light. Light was the gift she had hoped for, light to fill the world with nuance and possibility again. She had hidden from the sadness of his absence for so long that everything had been drained of color, of luminosity. She'd found the dullness a comfort, but she was emerging from it, she thought, and moving back into the world.

He had been her all, and his goodbye had seemed the end of everything. But it wasn't. It hadn't been. And longing had proven useless in the end. It brought her nothing but darkness. But light held out promise and she was determined to stand in it.

One student had an exhilarating experience reading this selection and felt that he'd made a real breakthrough. He had slowed down his reading and suddenly, emotions were being generated and he felt as if he was in dialogue with the text, that the words had a life and that they, as he put it, "…were going to do what they wanted to do as I approach them. All I have to do is wait, give them time."

He'd gotten into 'the zone,' where he wasn't measuring and judging himself. He wasn't outside looking in. He wasn't thinking about what to do. He was doing. He'd given himself time, read slowly, and focused on the story and the language. And that evoked emotions and ideas that were both personal to him, responsive to, and appropriate for, the material. This is a man whose natural style is aggressive and cigarette-smoke rough. He was surprised at how paying attention to the sounds of the language allowed him to access his softer side and connect to the delicate writing.

In the excerpt below, words are stacked on words, images crowd images; the language suggests precision, attention to detail. What point of view and tone emerge?

Text: AMBROSE

Ambrose fell asleep in his hotel in the early evening. He rose restlessly just before dawn. He rarely stayed up late enough or woke early enough to see the sunrise. This morning, though, the jetlag invigorated him. It rendered his nerves raw and receptive to even the gentle tonic effect of freshly squeezed orange juice on his unfurling senses.

Breakfast was served on a patio overhanging the bay. The far hills with their crumbling watchtowers and white houses crawling up from the sea—and nearer, less self-proclaiming cues like the rustic floor tiles and inefficient ways of the serving staff—told Ambrose that he was far from America, but in a milieu closer to home. Hints of early morning heat, tempered by a cooling breeze on his linen shirt, created a sensation of paradisical freshness. He ate a light breakfast and looked out at the water. His stomach and mind delightfully unencumbered, he felt ready to face the presentation he was giving at the conference in a few hours.

It went well. In face-to-face conversation, Ambrose often stammered ponderously as he sifted through the multiple ideas and half-formed witticisms that his imagination thrust on his attention. When he delivered a public presentation, he found that he became focused and fluid—at his best—witty and theatrical as well. So it was with his talk that day. This success was particularly gratifying to him now. He would be finishing his dissertation at Berkeley soon and was on the prowl for a job.[1]

Possible Point of View: *Precision holds things together*.
Possible Tone: *Crisp, sharp*.
Possible Personality: *Controlled, constrained*.

The previous selection is about a contemporary person in a contemporary intellectual milieu. Every story is set in a time and place and culture whose values and norms will help you shape the point of view and tone you'll give the book.

---

[1] Ari Juels, *Tetraktys* Texas: Emerald Bay Books, 2009.

6

Setting: Place, Time, Culture

Every story would be another story, and unrecognizable if it took up its characters and plot and happened somewhere else.

—Eudora Welty

The setting of a book roots us in the attitudes, behaviors and values of its particular place and time. A story about a contemporary intellectual enjoying her position in a university will have a different tone and point of view than one about farmers trying to survive in the American midwestern dust bowl of the 1930s. A book set in the New York City jazz scene of the 1950s will have a different tone and point of view than one set in a conservative small town of the same era.

Each setting gives us keys to the attitudes, behaviors and values of the period, place and culture in which the story takes place.

I had the pleasure of working with my daughter, Ariadne Meyers (aka Ari Meyers, *Kate and Allie*, *The Killing Secret*, *Dutch*) on a 'period' tween audiobook series, *Trixie Beldin*. The series was set in a 1940s rural town in New York's Hudson Valley. We loved the old-fashioned feel of the books which featured two young friends who solved local mysteries.

The main character, Trixie, was feisty and courageous and lived in a more innocent time when life for children was less complicated and they were not as exposed to adult issues. The language style was of the era, the narrative reflected the mores and values of the day. The characters' relationships and attitudes were less sophisticated than those found in contemporary tween books.

Ariadne gave the book an overall tone of *innocence*, consistent with the rural lifestyle and period. The point of view reflected the *gung-ho* personality of the main character, Trixie, that *life is a great adventure*. But knowing the time and place of the story, Ariadne modified that point of view, making it *life is a great adventure but respect societal limits*! A young female character today might have a similar but slightly different point of view such as, *life is a great adventure but test all limits*. And the tone of that book might be *edgy*, rather than *innocent*.

One way to get a good fix on the overall setting of a book you are working on is by referencing a film, a TV program or theatrical show set in its time period. Photos from that time and place can also give you a feel for a period or locale you've never experienced. You can also check with older folks for insight into the culture of their era.

Settings Workouts

The first-person book narrator in the following selection lives in the 1950s, when teachers and parents weren't focused on a kid's self-esteem, and kids didn't expect them to be. The story is set in an 'Oh boy, I'm in trouble!' era. This book narrator is certain his parents will side with his teacher rather than defend their son no matter that he was in the right.

Text: BAD DAY

Could this day get any worse? It's bad enough I'd gotten in trouble at school today. I didn't even throw that pencil; Bobby Johnson did.

I tried to tell Mrs. Tomlinson, but she wouldn't listen. Adults never listen!

It's bad enough being kept after school, but the teacher also gave me a note to bring home for my dad to sign.

I'm doomed! I'll probably be grounded for a week. There's no getting out of it. The only thing I can do now is ride my bike home from school real slow to avoid my punishment for a while.

But that jerk Billy Menken and his friends are coming the other way. Everyone thinks Billy is cool because he has a stingray bike with a banana seat and his parents let him grease his hair back. My mom won't let me slick my hair; she said it would make me look like a hoodlum.

Billy Menken is always chasing me and beating me up, but I can't figure out why. It seems like the rich kids are always steamed at us poor kids for some reason.

I've got no choice but to turn and peddle as fast as I can. My bike can't go faster than Billy's stingray, but I've got a little head start. I figure if I can just get around the corner and ditch behind Mr. Armstrong's hedges, I might just get away. [1]

Possible Point of View: *The world stinks.*
Possible Tone: *Repressed anger.*
Possible Personality: *Innocent, sensitive.*
Alternate Point of View: *This is hopeless.*
Alternate Tone: *Fearful.*
Alternate Personality: *Depressed.*

The next story takes us into the world of boxing, a world with its own rules and expectations of behavior. It's tough and personally challenging for the boxer. Let the language style, setting, and the culture of this world help you shape the story's point of view and tone.

---

[1] Text BAD DAY by Neil Mitchell.

Text: THE BOXER

Finally, I hear that damn bell ring. I'm six minutes into the first boxing match of my life at the 1977 New Jersey Golden Gloves Tournament. My opponent is confused. He doesn't know what to do with this six-foot three, one hundred and forty pound seventeen-year-old stick figure dancing in front of him. I have a pretty good left jab and so far it's kept him at bay, but it's just a ruse. I'm weak, and once he gets past my jab, I'll be helpless. And all the running around the ring it takes to keep him away from me is exhausting. My muscles are beginning to fail me. If he pours it on, he'll run me over for sure. I don't think I can keep this charade up for another three minutes.

A thick cloud of bluish smoke hangs suspended in the huge armory where this event is taking place. It's coming mostly from the pimped out old men in the crowd all decked out in their purple suits and wide brimmed hats, smoking cigars and betting on the outcome of each fight—putting money down on the empty chairs between them as if they're in Vegas. I go to my corner and fall onto the stool waiting for me, sweat drenching my hair and my boxing trunks, the cigar smoke scorching my lungs, making me breathe like I'm having an asthma attack.

My coach, who goes by the nickname Tex, jumps in front of me and squirts water into my gaping mouth. A former world-class boxer, now in his sixties, Tex is the archetype of a fighter. He has no cartilage left in his nose to speak of. His eyes are mere slits from the years of scar tissue build-up. His is a face one is not born with; it is a face that is earned. It is a face that's a source of pride and respect in the fighting world.[1]

Possible Point of View: *The world isn't fair.*
Possible Tone: *Tough but vulnerable.*
Possible Personality: *Brave.*

---

[1] Text THE BOXER by Neil Mitchell

Here's a selection set in a jazz club in the 1940s or '50s. The environment is exciting and enticing. It's a place where the rhythm and music
make you let go of your inhibitions. The language evokes the culture,
the period and its musical vibe. If you need references, there are many
photos of late-night clubs as well as movies set in that era. Use all your
techniques and make it swing.

Text: JAZZ

Sweet stepped his way down the block. A lived-it-all fifty
years old, Sweet moved across 116th street now with an
easy authority. Always the gentleman, his years in the clubs
had polished his style. His hat was slanted with a trajectory
pointing down towards his right eyebrow. From under that
hat, he could see the world in sharp focus, and he could hear
everything too. His body was loose, comfortable in its skin.

Now he was hearing the music, drums punctuating the night
and a tenor sax singing his name, "Sweet, Sweet, Sweet," from
behind a half-closed door. Shafts of rhythm poured out of that
door as if a personal greeting—"Hey Sweet man! Where you
been?" "Hey Sweet man, come on in."

Sweet smiled at the bouncer, gave him a slight nod of his
head and slid into the steamy, crowded room. The sax was
screaming for the bass now, urging it on in hot liquid swirls.
The bar was jammed tight and the women in spiked heels
leaned back, elbows balanced against the brash chrome of the
bar looking over everybody's head for someone, maybe for
anyone.

It was body-to-body on the dance floor too but with
enough room to keep the customers happy. There was enough
space for hips and shoulders and thighs that shimmied
and swayed and created dance as if for the first time, as if an
all-knowing cool God had created hips and shoulders and thighs
for just this purpose and this purpose only.

The piano man took his solo. Sweet could play better than that, good as the man was. He was just waiting for the right moment to glide up on that stage and slide onto the bench for one spectacular number! Sweet could sing too, with a velvety sound that drove every woman in the house crazy. He would start playing and singing and, like a magician, he'd do something hot and tempting, making something appear that had never been before. That's the way it was in his life too. He was cool, but you never quite knew what to expect, what trick he'd pull out of that hat of his.

Possible Point of View: *Life is great.*
Possible Tone: *Hot.*
Possible Personality: *Confident with swagger.*

The next text is an excerpt from Charles Dicken's *Great Expectations*, first published as a serial in 1860/1861. There are few recordings of English speech patterns from centuries prior to the twentieth century. Still, we've become accustomed—through public television productions, the BBC productions, and period piece movies, plays and recordings—to a certain restraint and formality in the speech patterns of earlier eras, unless the book narrator or characters are rowdy or boisterous.

Keeping the period in mind, the excerpt provides a good opportunity to see how the setting of this nineteenth century story influences the point of view and tone you discover for your reading.

The text lets you know that Pip, the first-person narrator, is looking back on his life. He has learned much about his youthful naiveté and expectations regarding people, money, class, power, love and his own prospects, and he brings all that to his remembrance. You may bring a 'stiff upper lip' interpretation to the material, or you may find that Pip has a good sense of humor about the past and is unrestrained in his descriptions. Alternately, you may find a wistful, softer tone to his memories. Let the setting inspire you. As with other book excerpts, approach this as a stand-alone piece. Your interpretation does not have to be the same as it would be if you were reading the entire book.

Text: *GREAT EXPECTATIONS*

My father's family name being Pirrip, and my Christian name Philip, my infant tongue could make of both names nothing longer or more explicit than Pip. So, I called myself Pip, and came to be called Pip.

I give Pirrip as my father's family name, on the authority of his tombstone and my sister—Mrs. Joe Gargery, who married the blacksmith. As I never saw my father or my mother, and never saw any likeness of either of them (for their days were long before the days of photographs), my first fancies regarding what they were like, were unreasonably derived from their tombstones. The shape of the letters on my father's, gave me an odd idea that he was a square, stout, dark man, with curly black hair. From the character and turn of the inscription, "Also Georgiana Wife of the Above," I drew a childish conclusion that my mother was freckled and sickly. To five little stone lozenges, each about a foot and a half long, which were arranged in a neat row beside their grave, and were sacred to the memory of five little brothers of mine—who gave up trying to get a living, exceedingly early in that universal struggle—I am indebted for a belief I religiously entertained that they had all been born on their backs with their hands in their trousers-pockets and had never taken them out in this state of existence.

Ours was the marsh country, down by the river, within, as the river wound, twenty miles of the sea. My first most vivid and broad impression of the identity of things, seems to me to have been gained on a memorable raw afternoon towards evening. At such a time I found out for certain, that this bleak place overgrown with nettles was the churchyard; and that Philip Pirrip, late of this parish, and also Georgiana wife of the above, were dead and buried; and that Alexander, Bartholomew, Abraham, Tobias, and Roger, infant children of the aforesaid, were also dead and buried; and that the dark flat wilderness beyond the churchyard, intersected with dykes and mounds and gates, with scattered cattle feeding on it, was the marshes; and that the low leaden line beyond, was the river; and that the distant savage lair from which the wind was rushing, was the sea; and that the small bundle of shivers growing afraid of it all and beginning to cry, was Pip.

Possible Point of View: *The past won't control me.*
Possible Tone: *Wistful or poignant or tender reverie.*
Possible Personality: *A dreamer who has had tough lessons to learn.*

Alternate Point of View: *I am no longer bound by my past.*
Alternate Tone: *Humorous, ironic.*
Alternate Personality: *A bit jaded.*

In the prior selection it's easy to envision the scene in vivid detail. That's because Dickens used powerful, evocative imagery.

7

Imagery

What You See is What You Get, as Long as You Can See It
—Barry Orms

We perceive the world through our senses. We see, hear, smell, touch, and taste. Imagery, in writing, is the language the author uses—the descriptive, evocative words that convey a mental picture of those sensory experiences. For the audiobook actor, it's vital to understand that a character's reaction to imagery is always shaped by the emotional context in which he or she experiences it. The image of a small room with a table, candle and cot might evoke a sense of peace and pleasure from the point of view of a person who loves to meditate, but to the person just released from prison it could be a dismaying, claustrophobic sight.

Imagery Workouts

The following workout, THE BEACH, will be presented twice. The text will be identical, but a different emotional context will be described for each reading. Be aware of how the different emotional contexts affect your response to the imagery.

For this first reading, assume the main character is returning to a beach where he spent a happy childhood.

Text: THE BEACH

The beach was still. No breeze. The salt smell of the sea air hung heavy in the night. The calls of the seabirds were the only sounds he heard as he walked near the softly lapping waves. Bits of broken shells were strewn along the shoreline, faintly white against the brown sand. He lifted one, its ridged back falling like the waves themselves, an endless repeating pattern. The night was cool and black, and the sky was strung with a million stars.

While working on this selection, one student (the ciga-rette-smoke-voiced gentleman) said that as he was reading, an image suddenly came to him of a man standing alone on the beach thinking of a time when he was a boy collecting seashells with his dad. The boy, of course, was him. He'd read slowly and the imagery in the little story had activated a loving memory which made him softly embrace the images of the beach and the shells. His point of view was, *I'll cherish this*, his tone, *reverent*.

Read the story again, but this time the emotional context is that the beach is a place of terrible memories, a place where a loved one had drowned. Be aware of how changing the emotional context changes how you respond to the images.

Text: THE BEACH

The beach was still. No breeze. The salt smell of the sea air hung heavy in the night. The calls of the seabirds were the only sounds he heard as he walked near the softly lapping waves. Bits of broken shells were strewn along the shoreline, faintly white against the brown sand. He lifted one, its ridged back falling like the waves themselves, an endless repeating pattern.

The night was cool and black, and the sky was strung with a million stars.

The following nonfiction excerpt is from Charles Darwin's, *The Voyage of the Beagle, Journal of Researches*. He is twenty-six years old and on the verge of extraordinary experiences and discoveries. He is a scientist, not a tourist seeking adventure. This workout gives you an opportunity to explore the imagery within the historical period when Darwin was working.

Text: APRIL 29TH

In the morning we passed round the northern end of Mauritius, or the Isle of France. From this point of view the aspect of the island equaled the expectations raised by the many well-known descriptions of its beautiful scenery. The sloping plain of the Pamplemousses, interspersed with houses, and colored by the large fields of sugar cane of a bright green, composed the foreground. The brilliancy of the green was the more remarkable because it is a color which generally is conspicuous only from a very short distance. Towards the center of the island groups of wooded mountains rose out of this highly cultivated plain; their summits, as so commonly happens with ancient volcanic rocks, being jagged into the sharpest points. Masses of white clouds were collected around these pinnacles, as if for the sake of pleasing the stranger's eye. The whole island, with its sloping border and central mountains, was adorned with an air of perfect elegance: the scenery, if I may use such an expression, appeared to the sight harmonious.

Given that Darwin was a scientist and of an older era, you could easily have chosen a point of view such as, *accuracy is critical*, with the tone being *precise*. But perhaps the poetry of his descriptions made you feel that he saw this from the point of view that *beauty is to be treasured*, and the tone was *enthralled*. Then again, maybe your point of view and tone were completely different.

In the following first-person selection, the setting is contemporary, and the context is clear; the character is working under a horrible boss. Use the context, the setting, the imagery and the language style, to help you nail your point of view and the tone of the story.

Text: LETICIA

I don't know why I thought it would work out. It seemed like a fabulous opportunity, but it turned into a nightmare; an absolute, go-home-and-stare-at-the-TV-for-hours-before-you-drag-yourself-to-your-bed nightmare. My friends say I'm depressed. Not clinically, but situationally. I am, you see, stuck in what should be a great job but which isn't. However, given the specter of the unemployment office, I cannot even think of quitting.

The problem is my boss. Leticia is extraordinarily looking, with the kind of beauty you first see as a gift of nature, then as a disguise meant to allow her to suck the blood from the unwitting who fall into her silky web. Dark haired, perfectly groomed, she keeps her fingernails long and painted deep red, using them to stab away at the flesh of some poor unsuspecting underling. Not literally of course, it's how she points them at you or at—as she calls it—your despicable work. She doesn't like to edit on the computer. She likes to print out your writing and use a felt tip red pen so she can slash big RED X's all over what you'd thought was a great first draft of an article. That pen has become an extension of her fingers, of her nails and of her bloody red soul.

My polished chrome and glass topped desk is strewn with crumpled papers, half-filled coffee cups whose cold contents are too gross to even be looked at, tissues ready to be wept into and a couple of bottles of herbal, over the counter, useless antidepressants. I feel so beaten down, so humiliated that despite my passion for the magazine world, I don't know how I can go on if I see those vicious, accusatory, evil nails pointing at me one more time.

The corner bar is my nightly warm and welcoming salvation; dim lights, old wooden tables with deep scratches crisscrossing their surfaces; a couple of slightly bleary eyed, but still upright alcoholics and a beefy barman with a full red beard hiding his red pockmarked cheeks. God, I love the joint!

Possible Point of View: *This is an insane nightmare.*
Possible Tone: *Mocking, ironic.*
Possible Personality: *Witty, irreverent.*
Alternate Point of View: *Everything in life is a hoot!*
Alternate Tone: *A frothy romp.*
Alternate Personality: *Exuberant, unabashed.*

In the opening paragraphs of *The Quest of the Silver Fleece*, by W.E.B. Du Bois, the young protagonist has left home for the first time, seeking an education. As he moves through the night, he encounters a girl who he discovers lives separate from society in a mysterious swamp. How does this powerful imagery affect you? What tone and point of view emerge in your reading? Allow your third person book narrator to reflect the emotions and experience of the young boy as he encounters the unexpected.

Text: *THE QUEST OF THE SILVER FLEECE*

Night fell. The red waters of the swamp grew sinister and sullen. The tall pines lost their slimness and stood in wide blurred blotches all across the way, and a great shadowy bird arose, wheeled and melted, murmuring, into the black-green sky.

The boy wearily dropped his heavy bundle and stood still, listening as the voice of crickets split the shadows and made the silence audible. A tear wandered down his brown cheek. They were at supper now, he whispered – the father and old mother, away back yonder beyond the night. They were far away; they would never be as near as once they had been, for he had stepped into the world. And the cat and Old Billy – ah, but the world was a lonely thing, so wide and tall and empty! And so bare, so bitter bare! Somehow, he had never dreamed of the world as lonely before; he had fared forth to beckoning hands and luring, and to the eager hum of human voices, as of some great, swelling music.

Yet now he was alone; the empty night was closing all about him here in a strange land, and he was afraid. The bundle with his earthly treasure had hung heavy and heavier on his shoulder; his little horde of money was tightly wadded in his sock, and the school lay hidden somewhere far away in the shadows. He wondered how far it was; he looked and harkened, starting at his own heartbeats, and fearing more and more the long dark fingers of the night.

Then of a sudden up from the darkness came music. It was human music but of a wildness and a weirdness that startled the boy as it fluttered and danced across the dull red waters of the swamp. He hesitated, then impelled by some strange power, left the highway and slipped into the forest of the swamp, shrinking, yet following the song hungrily and half forgetting his fear. A harsher, shriller note struck in as of many and ruder voices; but above it flew the first sweet music, birdlike, abandoned, and the boy crept closer.

The cabin crouched ragged and black at the edge of black waters. An old chimney leaned drunkenly against it, raging with fire and smoke, while through the chinks winked red gleams of warmth and wild cheer. With a revel of shouting and noise, the music suddenly ceased. Hoarse staccato cries and peals of laughter shook the old hut, and as the boy stood there peering through the black trees, abruptly the door flew open and a flood of light illumined the wood.

Amid this mighty halo, as on clouds of flame, a girl was dancing. She was black, and lithe, and tall, and willowy. Her garments twined and flew around the delicate moulding of her dark, young, half-naked limbs. A heavy mass of hair clung motionless to her wide forehead. Her arms twirled and flickered, and body and soul seemed quivering and whirring in the poetry of her motion.

As she danced, she sang. He heard her voice as before, fluttering like a bird's in the full sweetness of her utter music. It was no tune nor melody, it was just formless, boundless music. The boy forgot himself and all the world besides. All his darkness was sudden light; dazzled he crept forward, bewildered, fascinated, until with one last wild whirl the elf-girl paused. The crimson light fell full upon the warm and velvet bronze of her face—her midnight eyes were aglow, her full purple lips apart, her half hid bosom panting, and all the music dead. Involuntarily the boy gave a gasping cry and awoke to swamp and night and fire, while a white face, drawn, red-eyed, peered outward from some hidden throng within the cabin.

Possible Point of View: *This is an initiation, a threshold crossing.*
Possible Tone: *Mysterious, haunting.*
Possible Personality: *Innocent.*
Alternate Point of View: *There is danger here.*
Alternate Tone: *Cautious.*
Alternate Personality: *Reticent.*

This next text might first appear to be a thriller. Read through to the end so you'll know the context in which this vivid imagery is occurring and from whose point of view it's being told.

Text: HOLLYWOOD STORY

Throughout the corridors, lights of the emergency systems flicker on and off with no consistency. Jets of bright orange and blue sparks shoot from the smashed control panels and exposed wires that hung from the ceiling. Pipes protrude from the walls, some dripping a strange looking liquid, others shooting jets of boiling steam.

Few corpses have been left unscavenged; they are lying in puddles of blood where they've been attacked; flesh ripped away.

Suddenly, a figure enters the corridor, moving carefully and silently through the carnage. It wears a robotic mask and a metallic jacket with a design reminiscent of Star lord. Pulling a glowing device from its pant pocket, the figure scans the area, illuminating alien looking characters and cryptic, unrecognizable glyphs etched on the walls.

The figure continues moving forward until reaching a hatch with a small keypad, which it presses with the device until a hologram appears, indicating a decryption in progress. A distant sound, a low ominous hummm. roils down the corridors, coming from both directions. The figure turns, frantically searching for the source as the sound grows louder and louder, changing into a high pitched, vibrating screech.

The figure turns back to the hologram, pressing the device harder, urging the decryption process to move faster.

The screeching grows closer as new sounds reverberate through the halls: the sounds of feet running and scraping noises. The figure looks up and sees what appear to be several dull white figures clustered together, jostling around each other and moving closer with great speed. Where there should be faces, there are only milky white eyes. Grey mutated flesh hangs from their coral-like skeletons, as they move as one entity closing in from both sides. End scene.

There was a moment of quiet in the conference room as Rasheed stopped reading.

"So, what do you think?" he asked Jimmy, the young producer in charge of the film. Jimmy smiled and shook his head. "I think that shit sounds dope!" [1]

Possible Point of View: *Gotta grab them.*
Possible Tone: *Taut or hot.*
Possible Personality: *Clever, daring.*

Let's return to THE EXISTENTIAL COWBOY and the main character, Mike. We'll pick up where Mike brings his girlfriend Suzy, a flight attendant, with him on the trip he's making to explore the rural area he hopes to move to. They've just arrived at the local bar, the Dew Drop Inn. The period is the early '70s, but this town and its inhabitants have maintained their old timey, open cattle country ways, and they are vividly presented. You've established a tone and a point of view for the story in previous selections. Use those as you read and explore the imagery.

Text: THE EXISTENTIAL COWBOY (continued)

Suzy was with Mike one spring day, driving with the top down from Miami out to Davie, the small town in the middle of horse farms, cattle ranches and citrus groves way west of Ft. Lauderdale. This was the mecca of his dream-to-be, a place right out of a Western movie…unpaved dusty streets, feed stores, hitching posts, men and women in jeans and boots, the unmistakable earthy, warm smell of horses.

[1] Text excerpt from *Hollywood Story* a screenplay by Moses Williams.

Just outside of town was a roadhouse, the Dew Drop Inn, that he'd been told was a watering hole for the ranch owners and where Mike was determined to learn more about this way of life, soak up the culture and maybe a beer.

The Dew Drop Inn was the real deal, a western saloon complete with the iconic swinging, slatted doors and mournful country & western music floating out onto the street. Mike was half expecting a drunk to be thrown out the doors at any moment. As he began looking for a spot to park the Porsche, one of the roadhouse patrons stepped outside, no doubt summoned by the car's throaty exhaust. The guy had a large tan Stetson set back on his head and wore a colorful white western shirt with red piping that was tucked into Levi's that couldn't quite manage to clear the hump of his ample stomach. He stood absolutely still, eyeing first the Porsche, then Suzy whose top was almost as low as the roof of the car.

Mike parked and he and Suzy got out. Suzy was totally out of her element and as soon as she stepped from the car it hit her like the afternoon heat: she was a Valley girl, and the sight of this gnarled cowboy standing in the dusty parking lot staring her down was a little more than she was used to, notwithstanding the sometimes-mean-spirited drunks she had to deal with on her flights. The cowboy continued to eye them as they entered the bar. As they were getting accustomed to the relative dimness of the interior, the gnarled fellow entered behind them and sauntered over to the seat he had vacated at the bar. Then surprisingly, he turned to them, looked them up and down again and then motioned for them to come on over and sit. Now this place was really something…the bar was a long, glistening wooden slab, polished to a sheen from years of sopping up wet whiskey and beer. Behind it were old-timey gilt-edged mirrors with a huge smiling moose head looking down on them from above. Gaudy chandeliers that didn't provide much light hung from a blackened tin ceiling. The floors creaked, and the place smelled from cigarette butts, beer and cheap perfume. Mike loved it.[1]

As in The Existential Cowboy, travel to new places can be powerful experiences. In this story, Tanya, a young American tourist, is on her first trip outside of the United States. She's traveling in the Middle East during the 1960s. The sights and sounds are all new to her, and her excitement mounts as she encounters the visual beauty of a new land, until something disturbs that excitement.

Text: THE MARKET

They'd taken a small road as they headed towards the *shuk*—the central market in the small port city. Still an hour until noon, the sun was burning the narrow paths and heating the soft, damp air that smelled of sea and salt. The streets were deserted as Tanya, Peter and Dianna walked past the walled, silent courtyards—stone and concrete guardians of homes and inhabitants. In Brooklyn, where Tanya had lived her whole life, apartment buildings lined the streets. People gathered on stoops talking to each other, or they were rushing about. But here all was quiet—until they turned a corner and the market suddenly shimmered into existence, alive with sound and awash in color and light. Azure blues, gold, flashes of turquoise and silver burst into vibrant energy and life. Voices shouted from the entrances of shops and stalls as customers milled about—touching, feeling, weighing and measuring. It reminded her of the shops in her neighborhood where mostly women were bargaining and purchasing the items that kept their households running; but here it was more vibrant. Rolls of rainbow-colored fabrics flecked with gold threading were on display as was intricately carved jewelry: bracelets, earrings

---

[1] Text The Existential Cowboy by Ira Marks.

and rings flashed in the sun. A radio blared out a gorgeous, seductive rhythm of drumming as a high-pitched female voice undulated around the steady beats.

Travel, she'd always believed, expanded you; allowed you to be part of the great sweep of humanity. She looked around to share her feeling of excitement with her friends and suddenly, she realized that she was alone. Somehow, in the dazzle of the market, she'd wandered off, and now, she was one small person amidst a swirl of strangers. She felt a momentary rush of anxiety, a small clutch of fear for which she castigated herself. A fear of being alone had secretly haunted her for years, but she was older now, nearing thirty. Now was not the time to give in to it. Now was not the time for that clutch in her heart to take her over; now was the time to beat it back for as long as she could.

Possible Point of View: *Embrace it all.*
Possible Tone: *Youthful exuberance.*
Possible Personality: *Passionate.*

Each of the prior selections are filled with imagery and change as the stories progress. By reading from the book narrator's perspective, expressing the changing emotions—the joys, the fears, the shifting dynamics—you are moving the story forward, creating one of the most important aspects of audiobook acting: Experiential Immediacy.

PART *FOUR*

EXPERIENTIAL IMMEDIACY

The moment is the only thing that counts.

—Jean Cocteau, *Professional Secrets*

8

The Moment-to-Moment Reading

Drive change; don't wait for change to drive you.
—Jonathan Lockwood Huie

Creating Experiential Immediacy means giving a moment-to-moment reading—reacting to the changing events, emotions, challenges and conflicts as they occur in the story. It means creating a forward moving energy that keeps the listener eager to find out what happens next.

Experiential immediacy keeps your performance alive whether in first, second or third person. If hearing a book read without a point of view and tone is dull, listening to a production without experiential immediacy is about as exciting as listening to your mother's grocery list.

I was once flying to Los Angeles listening to an audio performance by an actor I was about to work with. I'd seen him in films and loved his work, so I was eager to hear the audiobook.

I put on headphones and was prepared for an exciting read. It was a tension filled book about a tough criminal enterprise and the actor was a natural for it, but there was a problem.

He'd read the book as if it was just one long 'tough' sentence. His performance never varied. There was no moment-to-moment change as the events, action and emotional content changed. The actor was great at playing a single role but hadn't mastered the shifting landscape of a good audiobook reading. Gentle moments, anxious moments, threatening moments, anticipation, fear, joy, acts of violence and acts of kindness all sounded the same. Tender love scenes sounded like a beatdown!

Still, listening to that production let me know how I could direct him into a more diverse and interesting read, one that was more responsive to the events and characters in the story. And once introduced to the technique of experiential immediacy, with a little in-studio practice, he gave our book a more exciting and layered performance. He used a *take no prisoners* point of view and a *hard-bitten* tone, but there was nuance, change, and responsiveness to the book's dynamics in his performance.

All the work you've been doing so far is geared to helping you create a moment-to-moment read. Let's look at a few specific components of experiential immediacy that you can apply to the skills you've acquired. As you explore the next sections remember: identify and apply your point of view and tone, be aware of language, culture, context, imagery. If you have trouble connecting, use any or all of your early techniques.

Read Aloud
    Slow it Down
        Do Nothing
            Note it
                Welcome the Unexpected
                    Don't Overdo it
                        Read as if to Someone You Know

Pacing

Pacing refers to the speed at which an action or activity unfolds. For the audiobook actor, pacing means how quickly or slowly you move a scene along to reflect what's happening in the story, both in action and emotion.

A book narrator's shift from a calm or pensive state to a more alert one, or to an excited or agitated one can be expressed not only by the change of intensity in the reading, but by a shift in pacing.

I worked with one audiobook actor whose pacing remained absolutely constant as a scene changed from a 'bucolic ride through the forest' into a 'heated battle.' The scene had been progressing at a leisurely pace; nothing requiring a different response was happening. Then the main character suddenly found himself in a situation that went from relaxed, to a skin prickling awareness of danger, and then to the intensity of fierce battle. But the scene fell flat because the actor didn't react to those changes. He should have shifted from a calm reading to a quickening 'on alert' awareness, and then into furious battle mode of 'heart pounding, fast action!' But he didn't, and so the scene was poorly paced and plodding.

At least until we stopped and discussed it.

The actor was very open to change and very creative. He loved trying a new approach and applied experiential immediacy to the scene. Though it sounds contradictory—because the scene had to speed up—he used the Slow it Down technique to discover his reactions to the material during a short, in-session rehearsal. When he was ready to record, the scene was vibrant and emotionally gripping, with pacing that picked up speed as the action and emotional intensity accelerated.

Pacing: Fiction Workouts

The following fantasy style story unfolds as the main character transitions from a slow, cautious, on-alert point of view to his accelerating realization of danger approaching, and then into fierce, fast-paced battle mode. Find the point of view and tone for the story, use all your techniques and allow the changes in the situation and character's responses to propel your pacing.

Text: SCLERID

Sclerid's troops moved slowly and cautiously into the Olglit's territory. A mountainous region, it was thick with forests of huge lumbering trees, wet moss and rocky outcroppings. The troops had moved under cover of darkness, only the white sliver of moon and distant gleam of a thousand stars illuminated the blackness of the night.

They'd hoped to pass through this terrain without a fight. His army was nimble, but they were few, far fewer than the Olglit's forces. Horses and men advanced slowly on the narrow path that crossed the mountain and cut through the looming forest, alert to every whisper of leaf, every breath on the wind. The crack of a branch was the first sign. Sclerid signaled his men to halt as he scanned the area.

Nothing. Perhaps it had been a bird. He signaled the troops forward.

Another crack of a branch.

He signaled the troops to halt again. "We come in peace," he called out. But only silence answered, an overwhelming silence, unnatural and heavy. Another crack of a branch, louder this time and then a whooping cry in a language Sclerid didn't understand but whose message was universal. A volley of arrows flew from the hills, sharp and swift. Horses screamed as arrows slid past or pierced flesh. Sclerid's horse reared as he signaled his troops to hold their positions behind the trees, rocks and boulders that stood on all sides as the Olglits rushed forward—giants with arrows and hammers hurled with unearthly force.

They ran down hills, terrible screams rising from their throats, weapons raining down terror. But Sclerid's mages were trained to control energy and reverse the forward motion of time. As the giants roared and flung weapons, their arrows suddenly stopped in the air. Hammers spun and returned to their stunned senders. Their leader howled in rage, signaling his men forward.

Bewildered, they streamed dutifully down from the mountain, rushing towards a time traveler's nightmare… stopped in space and flung up into the night, up, up to the moon and stars, and up into orbit like so many ancient, helpless asteroids, unable to change their course or momentum.

Olglit himself was spinning now, farther and farther away from land, farther from his troops until suddenly, the mountain was silent, as the remainder of his stunned and terrified forces slipped soundlessly back into the mountains, leaving the path open to Sclerid and his men.

Were you able to connect and give the piece the changes it calls for? If you're not satisfied, read it again, slowly, and let the story's shifting emotions and actions carry you forward.

The changes in the following text, though more internally generated, are as compelling to the main character in the story as anything occurring on a battlefield.

Text: THE CLERK

The clerk was alone. It was close to midnight and the minimart, just off exit 25 on Strikker Road, was empty and quiet. Bored, he pushed some of the candy bars on the counter from left to right then flipped absently through a magazine. He struck a match and was about to light a cigarette when the bell jangled on the door, and someone pushed it open. The clerk turned towards the doorway and nodded, but something about the man instantly felt wrong, something that made him itchy, made his skin prickle. The man standing in the entry didn't step in right away; he didn't move towards one of the aisles stocked with sodas, chips and stale coffee. The air, dull just a moment before, now gathered itself up, sharp and dangerous. The clerk flicked out the match and moved slowly towards the spot under the counter where he kept his—just in case there's trouble—baseball bat, his eyes steady on the man who was now walking directly towards him. The bell jangled again and this time a wiry, jumpy guy burst in and suddenly, all hell broke loose. The jumpy guy pulled a gun. The clerk moved fast, reaching for the bat as the first guy reached over the counter and grabbed him by his jacket.

Here's that same text with an example of pacing notes.

Text: THE CLERK (With Notes)

The clerk was alone. It was close to midnight and the minimart, just off exit 25 on Strikker Road, was empty and quiet. Bored, *PACE SLOWS A LITTLE, HIS ACTION IS CASUAL* he pushed some of the candy bars on the counter from left to right then flipped absently through a magazine. He struck a match and was about to light a cigarette when the bell jangled on the door, *PACING A LITTLE FASTER, MORE ALERT* and someone pushed it open. The clerk turned towards the doorway and nodded, but something about the man instantly felt wrong *PACING ACCELERATES, HE'S ON ALERT, ASSESSING*, something that made him itchy, made his skin prickle *PACING UP, SENSES DANGER*. The man standing in the entry didn't step in right away *PACING SLOWS, CLERK IS TAKING MEASURE*; he didn't move towards one of the aisles stocked with sodas, chips and stale coffee. The air, dull just a moment before, now gathered itself up, sharp and dangerous. *PACING SLOWER AS THE CLERK MOVES DELIBERATELY AND SLOWLY* The clerk flicked out the match and moved slowly towards the spot under the counter where he kept his—just in case there's trouble—baseball bat, his eyes steady on the man who was now walking directly towards him. The bell jangled again *PACING ACCELERATES* and this time a wiry, jumpy guy burst in and suddenly, all hell broke loose. *PACING ACCELERATES* The jumpy guy pulled a gun. The clerk moved fast, reaching for the bat as the first guy reached over the counter and grabbed him by his jacket.

Possible Point of View: *Never give in.*
Possible Tone: *Vigilant.*

Proper pacing not only reflects physical and emotional changes, it is key to communicating complex ideas. Pacing is as important when working on nonfiction as it is for fiction. Read too quickly and words and concepts may zip right past the listener. Read too slowly and the text can disintegrate into tiny shreds of disconnected thoughts.

Pacing: Nonfiction Workouts

Be sure that your pacing in the following nonfiction text allows you to convey the ideas in it clearly, within the point of view and tone you give it.

Text: HOW WE EVOLVED

Evolutionary theorists have often focused on what many see as a power principle. This viewpoint assumes that the challenges the human population faced as it developed were overcome strictly through power, mostly perceived as male dominant power: power over prey, power over perceived enemies, the power to overcome nature, to ensure mating rights, to protect a territory. This assumption provides us, perhaps unwittingly, with a perspective that views history through a single lens which, given its long entrenchment in the scientific community and popular imagination, eschews the view from the perspective of a differently oriented power definition. Cooperation, peace, and community building are brushed off as hippie navel-gazing, spiritual hoo-hah that must be intellectually dismissed or, in other words, overpowered. But increasingly, it seems highly likely that speech and social cohesion, that which powered social development, derives from mother-child communication and from females communicating as they gathered vegetables, roots and berries rather than via males in big game hunting parties. Those big game hunters had to be silent during large parts of a hunt or they'd come back empty handed. Berries on the other hand, don't run at the sound of a voice.

And neuroscience is adding new information to the mix with its understanding that our brains grew large because of energy provided by eating cooked foods. Cooking enables us to digest many more calories in a shorter period of time than does eating raw foods. And that increased energy led to our bigger brains. And who did the cooking? It was women the world over who, throughout history, did the daily cooking that likely helped fuel those big brains we humans developed. And it was women who did most, if not all, of the early childhood interaction with children. Cooing to a baby may be soft power, but empowering it is. Seeing the story of our species from this lens affords us a different viewpoint, one that recognizes our more peaceful, cooperative impulses as true power, equal to, and perhaps greater than, that of the power to overcome.

The Pause

You can use a pause—a little suspension in your reading—very effectively if you fill that pause with intent. You may pause at a particular place in your reading because something in the story makes the book narrator (and thus you) stop and think. It may be because a feeling or a thought needs to be processed. It could be that you pause to indicate that you are searching for just the right word. Maybe you stop to create suspense at a certain moment. Fill that pause with your intent, which you'll reflect in the words that follow.

The Pause: Workouts

In the next short text, GRACE, explore how you can use pauses to give this text a moment-to-moment reading.

Text: GRACE

Everyone seemed full of grace. Grace. Their voices. I could hear them so clearly and yes! Yes! Grace was in the sound of the rising chorus. Grace!

In the notated version following, the pauses, indicated by ellipses, show where the book narrator is searching for the right word, savoring it, thinking, then excitedly confirming her thought. A lot of action for a tiny reading.

Text: GRACE (with notes)

Everyone seemed...*SEARCHING FOR THE RIGHT WORD*...full of...
STILL SEARCHING THEN SUDDENLY REALIZES WHAT WORD SHE MEANS
grace... *ASSESSES THE CHOICE OF THAT WORD* Grace. Their voices...
PAUSES TO IDENTIFY THE SOUND I could hear them so clearly and
yes!.. *THINKING EXCITEDLY* Yes!.. Grace was in the sound of the
rising chorus. ... *PAUSES AGAIN TO SAVOR THE CHOICE AND EMBRACE THE WORD* Grace!

In the following text, no pauses are indicated. Use the tone *awe*, and the point of view that the book narrator is *amazed*. Read through and see how the pauses you give it can help express the tone and point of view.

Text: THE FORMULA

I stood there for several seconds. Could Laurie be correct? Had no one else discovered this formula? It was pure mathematics. Or was it? Had she discovered the profound structure, the mathematical substratum of not only the physical world but of consciousness itself? I've read voraciously but never have I seen anything like what Laurie had written. Yet was it possible? She was self-taught but what if what she was proposing was right? What if she'd hit on something that would transform the way we viewed everything?

An example of pause/pacing notes are given here. Pauses are indicated by ellipses.

Text: THE FORMULA (with notes)

I stood there for several seconds…Could Laurie be correct?… *ASSESSING THE POSSIBILITY*… Had no one else discovered this formula? It was pure mathematics… *DAWNING THOUGHT* Or was it?…Had she_discovered the profound structure, the mathematical substratum of not only the physical world but of consciousness itself?… *STUNNED* I've read voraciously but never have I seen anything like what Laurie had written. … Yet was it possible? She was self-taught but what if what she was proposing was right? *AMAZING* What if she'd hit on something that would transform the way we viewed … *THRILLED* everything?!

Pauses are essential for comedy, in which timing is critical. A tenth of a second can be the difference between getting the laugh or falling on your face. I was working on a section of a comedic audiobook that had three characters reading different lines, followed by the book narrator saying the two final words. The timing for the pause between the last sentence and the book narrator's two words was critical.

I'd come up with a series of edits for that section and had been working on that minute of material for nearly an hour with my engineer/editor, Dave LeVan. The Executive Producer from the publishing company was in the studio as well. Actually, Dave and the Exec were not happy when I said we needed more work on the end of the scene, which was about ten seconds of material. "Use take 22 for the first seven words," I said. "Then use the next six words from take 18, give it a split-second pause, then use the final two words from take 23 and it will be a laugh out loud moment."

That audiobook was produced in the dinosaur days—before digital recording and editing. We were working with reel-to-reel analog tapes and using a razor to slice the tape and then we'd splice it together to create the edits. Well, Dave would slice and splice. I would comment.

"Noo…" I'd say after he'd spliced, "make it a tiny bit longer on the pause." So, Dave would add a very small bit of tape, and re-splice it.

"Ummm…" I'd say, "make the pause a tiny bit shorter." He'd redo it and I'd say, "That's not exactly right. A teeny tiny bit longer on the pause."

Naturally Dave began grumbling. So did the Exec, but I refused to give up. I insisted that the length of the pause was critical. The right timing would make the joke! The wrong timing? No joke.

After several more tries, Dave nailed it.

Much later, as we were listening to the program from start to finish, Dave, the Exec and I broke out in raucous laughter at just the spot I'd made everyone crazy with my 'tiny bit more,' 'tiny bit less' corrections. That little pause we'd worked so hard to perfect, that just the right teeny bit of empty space was not empty. You 'heard' the book narrator thinking, deciding and then landing on the final words!

Beats

Beats are consistent sections of thought or action. Beats change as the action or emotional content changes. Perhaps there's a shift in the book narrator's attention. Perhaps a new idea suddenly occurs to her. A new beat might arise because there's a turn in the plot or a change of setting or plan.

The moment-to-moment reading allows you to stay aware of, and be sensitive to, when a beat shifts.

Beat shifts are essential in all of the arts. Other than music designed to put us into a meditative state, musical compositions shift and change all the time. It's the same for theater and film. We'd zone out watching a show or movie where the action never shifted. The beat may go on, but it always changes.

Beats Workout

Let's go back to THE MARKET story. In this version there are no paragraph breaks to indicate a beat change. Change the beat where you think the book narrator makes a shift in focus.

Text: THE MARKET (with no paragraph breaks)

They'd taken a small road as they headed towards the *shuk*—the central market in the small port city. Still an hour until noon, the sun was burning the narrow paths and heating the soft, damp air that smelled of sea and salt. The streets were deserted as Tanya, Peter, and Dianna walked past the walled, silent courtyards—stone and concrete guardians of homes and inhabitants. In Brooklyn, where Tanya had lived her whole life, apartment buildings lined the streets. People gathered on stoops talking to each other, or they were rushing about. But here all was quiet—until they turned a corner and the market suddenly shimmered into existence, alive with sound and awash in color and light. Azure blues, gold, flashes of turquoise and silver burst into vibrant energy and life. Voices shouted from the entrances of shops and stalls as customers milled about—touching, feeling, weighing, and measuring. It reminded her of the shops in her neighborhood where mostly women were bargaining and purchasing the items that kept their households running; but here it was more vibrant. Rolls of rainbow-colored fabrics flecked with gold threading were on display as was intricately carved jewelry: bracelets, earrings and rings flashed in the sun. A radio blared out a gorgeous, seductive rhythm of drumming as a high-pitched female voice undulated around the steady beats. Travel, she always believed, expanded you; allowed you to be part of the great sweep of humanity. She looked around to share her feeling of excitement with her friends and suddenly, she realized that she was alone. Somehow, in the dazzle of the market, she'd wandered off, and now, she was one small person amidst a swirl of strangers. She felt a momentary rush of anxiety, a small clutch of fear for which she castigated herself. A fear of being alone had secretly haunted her for years, but she was older now, nearing thirty. Now was not the time to give in to it. Now was not the time for that clutch in her heart to take her over; now was the time to beat it back for as long as she could.

Here's the story with one interpretation of where beat changes belong.

Text: THE MARKET (with beats)

They'd taken a small road as they headed towards the *shuk*—the central market in the small port city. Still an hour until noon, the sun was burning the narrow paths and heating the soft, damp air that smelled of sea and salt. *NEW BEAT* The streets were deserted as Tanya, Peter and Dianna walked past the walled, silent courtyards—stone and concrete guardians of homes and inhabitants. *NEW BEAT* In Brooklyn, where Tanya had lived her whole life, apartment buildings lined the streets. People gathered on stoops talking to each other, or they were rushing about. But here all was quiet—until they turned a corner and the market suddenly shimmered into existence, alive with sound and awash in color and light. *NEW BEAT* Azure blues, gold, flashes of turquoise and silver burst into vibrant energy and life. Voices shouted from the entrances of shops and stalls as customers milled about—touching, feeling, weighing and measuring. It reminded her of the shops in her neighborhood where mostly women were bargaining and purchasing the items that kept their households running; but here it was more vibrant. *NEW BEAT* Rolls of rainbow-colored fabrics flecked with gold threading were on display as was intricately carved jewelry: bracelets, earrings and rings flashed in the sun. A radio blared out a gorgeous, seductive rhythm of drumming as a high-pitched female voice undulated around the steady beats. *NEW BEAT* Travel, she always believed, expanded you; allowed you to be part of the great sweep of humanity. She looked around to share her feeling of excitement with her friends and suddenly she realized that she was alone. *NEW BEAT* Somehow, in the dazzle of the market, she'd wandered off, and now, she was one small person amidst a swirl of strangers. She felt a momentary rush of anxiety, a small clutch of fear for which she castigated herself. A fear of being alone had secretly haunted her for years, but she was older now, nearing thirty. Now was not the time to give in to it. Now was not the time for that clutch in her heart to take her over; now was the time to beat it back for as long as she could.

The following workouts allow you to use all the experiential immediacy techniques you've been working with. For each, see what tone and point of view you come up with.

Experiential Immediacy Workouts

In this story, the context is that main character, Jonah, is in an extremely dangerous situation, and he is very alert to the danger he faces. As the third person book narrator, you can get inside Jonah's head, express his innermost thoughts, the changing focus of his attention and his reactions as the scene unfolds. Is he thinking or moving slowly? When is he frightened? Cautious? Where does the story speed up or slow down? When does he pause and why? When is his attention shifting? When is he making a decision? Whether you tell the story from the point of view of an outside viewer, or you are directly reflecting what Jonah is experiencing, giving it a moment-to-moment reading makes it compelling.

As you create experiential immediacy in the reading, you draw your listener more deeply into the story as you give them the ups, the downs, the tensions, the fears, the excitements that are happening as they occur. As a reminder, you don't have to be big to do this. Audiobooks are not the medium for big, loud dramatics. You can create all the dramatic impact you want on a more intimate level. If you find you are creating a scene more suited to the stage, keep your same responses, but contain them, make them 'ear friendly.'

Text: JONAH

Jonah moved silently and slowly up the path towards the shack. This was the one opportunity he would have, and he knew he'd better not blow it. He listened for any hint of sound: for any telltale laughter from inside, the "chht" of a match being struck, the scraping of a chair on the rough-hewn floorboards of the shack. But all was still. Jonah reached the door and stopped for a moment… listening again. The absence of sound was no guarantee the shack was empty. There was no telling who or what was waiting inside. No harm in caution.

The place was old and beaten down. Sitting off the main road, it stank of old cigars and other men's fear. He'd been there before, when the deal was supposed to have gone down, and he knew the layout—the wooden table, three chairs, lousy sofa and boxes everywhere.

He pushed the door in quickly and moved inside—gun drawn—on the alert. He scanned the room for the slightest sign of movement...a shadow...a flicker of light. He sniffed the air for the scent of fear floating on a breeze…or the acrid hint of a cigarette hastily extinguished. There was none. He held his breath to listen for any new sound...the thump of a heartbeat… a stolen breath…He heard nothing but the electric hum of an overhead light bulb.

Slowly he relaxed. Not enough to put the gun away or to release the inner spring in his brain that would propel his body into action if necessary, but enough that he could breathe again and see what they'd left behind. A sign maybe, an indication of their next move. Because there would be one. They would have left him one. He was sure of that.

Possible Point of View: *This is life and death.*
Possible Tone: *Urgent.*
Possible Personality: *Intense.*

Following is the JONAH story, with notes demonstrating one interpretation of moment-to-moment responses.

Text: JONAH (with notes)

Jonah moved silently and slowly up the path towards the shack *PACING SLOW... ON ALERT FEELING CAUTIOUS* This was the one opportunity he would have, and he knew he'd better not blow it. *NEW BEAT* He listened for any hint of sound: *PAUSE, SHIFT OF ATTENTION TO LISTENING* for any telltale laughter from inside, *SLOWS, LISTENING TO SEE IF THERE'S ANYONE THERE* the "chht" of a match being struck, *PAUSE* the scraping of a chair on the rough-hewn floorboards of the shack. *PAUSE...REASSURING HIMSELF* But all was still. *NEW BEAT* Jonah reached the door and stopped for a moment...listening again. *PAUSE THEN PACING UP...REALIZING HE CAN'T RELAX*

The absence of sound was no guarantee the shack was empty. No use in taking any unnecessary risks. There was no telling who or what was waiting inside. No harm in caution. *NEW BEAT, TAKING IN THE SIGHT AND SMELLS*

The place was old and beaten down. Sitting off the main road, it stank of old cigars and other men's fear. He'd been there before, when the deal was supposed to have gone down, and he knew the layout the wooden table, three chairs, a lousy sofa and boxes everywhere. *NEW BEAT. PACING ACCELERATES GEARING UP TO REACT QUICKLY.*

He pushed the door in quickly and moved inside – gun drawn—on the alert. He scanned the room for the slightest sign of movement... *NEW BEAT. SMALL PAUSES AS JONAH SEARCHES FOR ANY TELLTALE SIGNS. CAN'T LET DOWN HIS GUARD.* a shadow... *TINY PAUSE* a flicker of light.... *TINY PAUSE* He sniffed the air for the scent of fear drifting on a breeze... or the acrid hint of a cigarette hastily extinguished. There was none. He held his breath to listen for any sound... *PACING UP AS HE QUICKLY LISTENS*

AGAIN FOR SOUNDS. the thump of a heartbeat... a stolen breath....
He heard nothing but the electric hum of an overhead light
bulb. *NEW BEAT.*

Slowly he relaxed. *DECELERATE.* Not enough to put the gun
away, or to release the inner spring in his brain that would
propel his body into action if necessary, but enough so that he
could breathe again and see what they'd left behind. *TENSION
LOWERS, RELIEF. A MOMENT TO ASSESS WHAT'S NEXT.* A sign maybe,
an indication of their next move. Because there would be one.
They would have left him one. *NEW BEAT. WARY, BUT FEELING
POWERFUL.* He was sure of that.

Experiential immediacy is just as powerful when the action is happening inside someone's mind. *Notes from Underground*, by Fyodor
Dostoevsky, presents a tormented, first-person narrator. Here he is describing himself to an unseen, 'distinguished' audience. For this workout, it's not necessary to have read the book. Approach it as a stand-
alone piece.

Text: *NOTES FROM THE UNDERGROUND*

I am a sick man...I am a spiteful man. I am an unattractive
man. I believe my liver is diseased. However, I know nothing at all about my disease, and do not know for certain what
ails me. I don't consult a doctor for it, and never have, though
I have a respect for medicine and doctors. Besides, I am extremely superstitious, sufficiently so to respect medicine, anyway (I am well-educated enough not to be superstitious, but I
am superstitious). No, I refuse to consult a doctor from spite.
That you probably will not understand. Well, I understand it,
though. Of course, I can't explain who it is precisely that I am
mortifying in this case by my spite: I am perfectly well aware
that I cannot "pay out" the doctors by not consulting them; I
know better than anyone that by all this I am only injuring

myself and no one else. But still, if I don't consult a doctor it is from spite. My liver is bad, well—let it get worse.

Here's the same text with notes from one interpretation. These notes are more extensive than you'd normally be using. They demonstrate how much can happen when you take your time and connect to a story. A few pauses can reveal so much inner thought.

Text: *NOTES FROM THE UNDERGROUND* (with notes)

I am a sick man...I am a *PAUSE, LOOKING FOR WORD* spiteful man. I am *PAUSE...REACHING FOR DETRIMENTAL WORD.* an *SPITS THE NEXT WORDS AS IF DARING THE LISTENER TO AGREE.* unattractive man. *PAUSES FOR A SECOND AS IF WAITING TO SEE IF THERE WILL BE A RESPONSE...THEN ACCELERATES...HURRIES ON TO STOP ANY COMMENT.*

I believe my liver is diseased. However, I know nothing at all about my disease, and *HESITATES BECAUSE HE HAS TO CONFESS...* do not know for certain what ails me. I don't consult a doctor for it, and never have, though I have a respect for medicine and doctors. Besides, I am extremely superstitious, *STOPS, FOR A SECOND, FEELING COMPELLED TO EXPLAIN...* sufficiently so to respect medicine, anyway (I am well-educated enough not to be superstitious, but I am superstitious). *PAUSE TO PUT HIS THOUGHTS TOGETHER FOR A BEAT, THEN RECONFIRMS HIS FIRST SELF-DESCRIPTION. NEW BEAT.* No, I refuse to consult a doctor from spite. *HE STOPS AND BEGINS TO FIND IT TWISTEDLY AMUSING AND WITH WRY LAUGHTER, ACCELERATES, AND RACES THROUGH HIS NEXT WORDS*

That you probably will not understand. Well, I understand it, though. Of course, I can't explain *SLOWS, A MOMENT OF REALITY, REALIZING THAT HE DOESN'T KNOW WHO HIS SPITE IS AIMED AT* who it is precisely that I am mortifying *NEW BEAT. THE SNIDE AMUSEMENT IS GONE.* in this case by my spite: I am perfectly well aware that I cannot... *AGAIN, SEARCHES FOR A WORD* "pay out" the doctors by not consulting them; *ACCELERATES, BRUSHING IT*

OFF, COVERING THE WEAKNESS HE JUST SHOWED I know better than anyone that by all this I am only injuring myself and no one else. But still, if I don't consult a doctor *SLOWS, DRAWS OUT THE NEXT WORDS FOR EFFECT* it is from… *PAUSES, HITS NEXT WORD FAST AND HARD.* spite. My liver is *SPITS NEXT WORDS* bad, well let it get worse.

Experiential immediacy, the moment-to-moment reading, enables you to convey the rising and falling tensions, and twists and turns in the narrative from a story's opening to its conclusion. It enables you to express all the changes in thinking and emotion of the characters who people that story, and whose goals and experiences drive it forward.

PART FIVE

CHARACTERS AND CHARACTER VOICES

There are no ordinary people.
—C.S. Lewis

9

Characters

If I try to be like him, who will be like me?
—Yiddish Proverb

One of the great joys of audiobook acting is that unless it's a multi-cast production, you get to play all the characters in the book. You play the lovers, the haters, the mobsters and the cops; you play people of all ages, ethnicities and genders. You'll give voice to your inner nerd, your inner hottie, your inner cowboy or cowgirl and perhaps—if you're lucky—your inner fire breathing, green saliva dripping, extra-terrestrial named Goth! You can play characters you'd never have the opportunity to play in other media because for audiobooks, you are not limited by your gender, age, ethnicity or physical appearance. You'll usually be reading the book narrator and main character in your own voice. It's all those other characters in the book you'll be voicing that give you the opportunity to flex your character portrayal muscles.

Our voices express much about us—our personality, gender, age, ethnicity, nationality. We often feel as if we know a lot about someone just by hearing them speak. For the audiobook actor, knowing who your characters are is the first step in developing their Character Voices.

The author gives you information about the characters' ages, backgrounds, environments and personalities in the book, (even Goth's). Combine this with your own creativity and you are in 'tour de force' land.

Your interpretations can be subtle, giving just a touch of personality and vocal distinction, or you can give each character a very distinctive voice, making your reading sound like a multi-cast production.

Because a book will usually have a lot of characters to voice, make a list of the book's characters (Character List) and give each a simple Character Key—a list of the character's key traits. This will help you define and remember who's who.

The Character Key

1. Character's name.

2. Age. (If age is not revealed, use information such as work history, activity level, and attitudes, that might indicate an era in which the character was born.)

3. Ethnicity, nationality, or region influencing accent.

4. Accent.

5. Profession or job.

6. Personality traits: adventurous, shy, lonely, gregarious, bold, daring, fearful, intolerant, overly kind, self-effacing, powerful, loves challenges, hates challenges, joyous, nervous, pompous, self-righteous, domineering, judgmental, funny, conflicted, intimidating, etc. These may be noted by the author or determined by how you interpret the character's personality.

A Character Key can be as simple as the following:

ALICIA: 30, Puerto Rican, gentle, professor, very curious, enjoys research.

CARL: 50, Southern, Black, warm personality, articulate politician, loves a challenge.

EVA: 45, Midwestern, White, nervous, hesitant, a grade-school teacher.

Character Key Workouts

For main characters you'll find a great deal of information in the book. But even with just a little information you can create a Character Key. Create one for each of the five characters below based on the information in the brief text given for each.

JAMES: James droned on and on. Someone tried to interject a comment, but James didn't notice. Hands over his rather expansive stomach, he went on and on, impervious to any sign of his listeners' boredom.

JOE: Joe was born tough. City bred on the streets of New York's hard-knock Hell's Kitchen, he used speech like a hammer going after a reluctant nail. His eyes were dark and tough, too.

OLIVIA: He saw Olivia the minute she entered the room. He loved the way she moved—slowly and languidly—smiling as she passed the other guests. She was only twenty-eight, but very ambitious and on track to be partner in one of the top law firms in the city. The hint of Georgia lingered in her speech, alluring and redolent of breezes and magnolia. Good lord, he thought as she reached him and took his arm, What had he done to deserve her?

AVERY: College was transformative for Avery, affording the intellectual life they had hoped for. They were a bio major, but Saturday nights were reserved for doing stand-up comedy. Comedy by night, potentially breakthrough bio research by day.

LILA: Her voice darted hopefully around the edge of the conversation in a fruitless effort to join in and then simply floated away, lost in the tinkle of glasses. Soon she herself faded into the laughter, into the sounds of other people's engagement.

Sample Character Keys for James, Joe, Olivia, Avery, and Lila.

JAMES: Male, 50s, portly, any ethnicity, boring, unaware of his dulling effect.

Alternate Character Key: Male, 50s, portly, any ethnicity, dull but desperately wants to be liked.

JOE: Male, 30s, aggressive, any ethnicity, tough as nails, 100% sure of himself.

Alternate Character Key: Male, 40s, any ethnicity, hostile, covers his vulnerability with a tough façade.

OLIVIA: Female, 28, Black, Southern, gorgeous, slight southern accent, aware of her looks but doesn't try to use them, smart and caring.

Alternate Character Key: Female, 28, Black, Southern, gorgeous, slight southern accent, will of iron, fiercely ambitious.

AVERY: Non-binary, 20, smart, passionate about their research, loves to joke and laugh.

Alternate Character Key: Non-binary, 20, intense, uses comedy as a release from the drive they feel to succeed at their work.

LILA: Female, 20s, petite, shy, lonely, White (any region), socially inept but longs to fit in.

Alternate Character Key: Yours to fill in; I only see her that way.

Let's return to the JAZZ text. You've given the story a tone and point of view and set it in its time period. Now give Sweet his Character Key.

Text: JAZZ

Sweet stepped his way down the block. A lived-it-all fifty years old, Sweet moved across 116th street now with an easy authority. Always the gentleman, his years in the clubs had polished his style. His hat was slanted with a trajectory pointing down towards his right eyebrow. From under that hat, he could see the world in sharp focus, and he could hear everything too. His body was loose, comfortable in its skin.

Now he was hearing the music, drums punctuating the night and a tenor sax singing his name, "Sweet, Sweet, Sweet," from behind a half-closed door. Shafts of rhythm poured out of that door as if a personal greeting! "Hey Sweet man! Where you been?" "Hey Sweet man, come on in."

Sweet smiled at the bouncer, gave him a slight nod of his head and slid into the steamy, crowded room. The sax was screaming for the bass now, urging it on in hot liquid swirls. The bar was jammed tight and the women in spiked heels leaned back, elbows balanced against the brash chrome of the bar looking over everybody's head for someone, maybe for anyone.

It was body-to-body on the dance floor too but with enough room to keep the customers happy. There was enough space for hips and shoulders and thighs that shimmied and swayed and created dance as if for the first time, as if an all-knowing cool God had created hips and shoulders and thighs for just this purpose and this purpose only.

The piano man took his solo. Sweet could play better than that, good as the man was. He was just waiting for the right moment to glide up on that stage and slide onto the bench for one spectacular number! Sweet could sing too, with a velvety sound that drove every woman in the house crazy. He would start playing and singing, and like a magician, he'd do some-thing hot and tempting, making something appear that had never been before. That's the way it was in his life too. He was cool, but you never quite knew what to expect, what trick he'd pull out of that hat of his.

Possible Character Key:

SWEET: About 50, male, Black, lives in Harlem, New York. A musician, cool, confident, a charmer.

Write a Character Key for High School Assistant Principal (AP) Go based on the following text.

Text: AP GO

Like every other guy on campus, I hated AP Go. And I, like every guy on campus, had to restrain himself from grabbing and kissing her. She had the body of a go-go dancer and the heart of a lizard. Every day she wore her hair in a ponytail that fell like a black whip down to her (according to Russ Hanzlik, the physiology teacher) L4 (lumbar 4), a skirt that revealed a sufficient portion of her ex-ballet dancer's thighs and black leather boots that snaked up and over her knees. She looked more like someone who ran an escort service than she did the assistant principal of a high school in the second wealthiest community in California.

Because AP Go's words were, as usual, direct, terse and mean spirited, I felt as if I had to defend both Maureen and myself.[1]

Possible Character Key:

AP GO: Mid to late 30s, Korean American, High School Assistant Principal tough, sharp, mean-spirited. No accent.

Once you know who your characters are, it's time to give them their voices.

---

[1] Dennis Danziger, *A Short History of a Tall Jew*. Deal Street Press, 2010.

10

Character Voices for Adults

The human voice is the organ of the soul.
—Henry Wadsworth Longfellow

Voices are identifiable by their sound and by the communication style of the speaker. The vocal elements in our speech patterns—our pacing, cadence, articulation, accents and others described in this chapter—can reveal much about who we are. An introverted person speaks quite differently than a super-confident, extroverted one. A fast talking 'motormouth' communicates differently than a slow, 'hey-man-don't-rush-me' character. We identify people by these kinds of patterns all the time; it's what makes a good impersonator good. They don't just capture the sound of someone's voice, they also capture the speech pattern of that individual, his or her essence.

In the JAZZ text, Sweet was described as 'a gentleman,' and as 'cool.' It says that he moved with 'easy authority,' he 'smiled' at the bouncer in the club and he 'glided' up to the stage. From those references, his Possible Character Key described him as cool, confident, and a charmer. The text also noted that he could sing and his voice had a 'velvety' sound. Given the personality described, and the reference to his vocal sound, his Character Voice would likely be warm with an emphasis on open vowels. The pitch of his voice could be baritone, and some of the vocal elements you'd use might be moderate pacing, and a smooth, melodic cadence.

The text of the AP GO story described her words as direct, terse and mean spirited. The author further notes her ponytail falling, 'as a black whip.' With that information, her Possible Character Key described her personality as tough, sharp, mean-spirited. If AP Go had dialogue, (and she will in a later section of the story) you'd likely make her Character Voice fast paced with an emphasis on consonants, not with moderate pacing and open vowels like Sweet's voice. Her vocal pitch isn't noted but comparing her ponytail to a whip might give you the idea of the high, sharp sound of a crack of a whip, which could make you think of a sharp, high-pitched voice.

You can give your characters their identifiable Character Voices by making sure their voice reflects their Character Key. The following Vocal Elements can be used to communicate a lot about your characters. Mix and match them and see how they help you infuse a Character Voice with that individual's personality. You may think of other characters for whom these vocal elements will be applicable, and you may come up with different vocal elements. The more you have in your arsenal, the more options you'll have to diversify your Character Voices.

Vocal Elements

Pitch

Everyone's voice has a natural pitch—the highness or lowness of that voice. Of course we vary our pitch when we speak. If we didn't, we'd sound robotic, but the general, baseline pitch of someone's voice can quickly convey important information about that character.

1. Gender. Men's voices are usually lower than women's.

2. Age. The pitch of a voice changes as its owner ages. Children have high voices which lower as they get older.

3. Perceived social position, especially power and authority. Though we often think of lower pitched voices as being more authoritative, don't get locked into a generalization. Actor Marlon Brando, for example, who commanded the screen, had a high-pitched voice. Big tall Abe Lincoln is reported to have had a softer, higher voice than we might imagine for his stature and authority. My mother's voice was so low pitched, that telemarketers addressed her as "Sir."

Cadence

The rhythm of our speech, the way our words flow and their pacing, how our pitch changes when our voice goes up and down, the melody of our speech, is what cadence refers to.

Everyone has a natural cadence. It's most easily recognizable in accents, think Southern drawl, Irish lilt, etc. In addition to where a character comes from, you can use cadence to reveal personality traits. For example:

1. A timid soul might say a few words quickly with an ascending pitch, pause, and then rush a few more words out, his pitch descending now as he nervously gets to the end of a phrase.

2. A boring character might speak with a flat pattern—very little pitch variation and a static rhythm that drones on with no changes.

3. An aggressive character might 'punch' the words in sentences, while dropping their pitch at the same spot for emphasis.

4. A smug character might use a descending cadence to imply that his word was the ultimate thought.

Upspeak

Ending an affirmative sentence as if it's a question.
You can use upspeak to convey:

1. A character who lacks confidence.

2. Someone in an inferior position at work or in a relationship.

3. Someone using upspeak to try to disarm or trick a potential opponent.

Breathiness

Breathiness, a lot of air in the vocal sound, is often used to convey sexiness in women (think Marilyn Monroe). It can convey an older or infirm person. But don't get stuck in the expected. A very tough person with a breathy voice can have an insidious, scary quality.

Character Voice Workout

Using the Character Keys you created for James, Joe, Olivia, Avery and Lila, and the vocal elements and speech patterns described so far, give each person a Character Voice. Record each voice reading the following text, THE MEETING.

Text: THE MEETING

I thought that it might be appropriate to attend last night's meeting. It was the school board meeting, and members of my family have attended the local high school for many years, and I do have my concerns. There is great disagreement regarding the allocation of funds. A number of individuals believe we should be raising money to improve the football field, build better stands, and whatever else they think important.

I want to make my thoughts known, that if money is to be raised, it should be to improve our science department. That is the future. I know that participation in sports is important, but we must prepare our students with the knowledge that will lead all of them to bright futures.

Listen to your recordings. Do the Character Voices you've created sound different from each other? Do they convey their Character Keys? If not, rework and re-record them until you're satisfied you've nailed them. Keep the final recordings; these Character Voices can become the start of your Character Voice reference file. And with just a bit of tweaking, some of the voices you develop can fit the bill for new characters.

Pace

Pace is the rate of speed at which something takes place. For the purposes of Character Voices, it's the pace at which the character speaks. Whether it's fast, slow, or somewhere in between, everybody has a natural vocal pacing, and, as with the examples of AP Go and Sweet, their pacing can be used to reflect a character's personality traits:

1. One character can speak quickly because they want to convey that they're a busy, high-powered exec with little time to waste.

2. Another is so smart, and thinks so quickly, that their pace goes at lightning speed.

3. You can make a character a slow speaker to convey a very deliberative, thoughtful person, or someone who is ill.

4. Another slow talker may be full of himself and speak very slowly and deliberately because he thinks his every word is a precious gem.

5. You can use a slow, hesitant pace because a character is shy and fearful that people will think what he or she is saying is not worth hearing.

Of course a character's vocal pacing may change when a situation arises that makes them speak more quickly or slowly, but giving them a natural pace sets their baseline.

Articulation

The manner in which you use your tongue, lips, teeth and jaw to produce a speech sound.

1. Precise articulation can convey a very erudite individual.

2. Exaggerated articulation, purposely separating and emphasizing syllables for example, can convey snobbery, or disdain for a listener.

3. Sharp articulation, with emphasis on consonants, can indicate nastiness.

4. Imprecise articulation, slurring, can indicate speech problems, a medical condition, or inebriation.

Vocal Fry

An elongation of certain syllables and vowels as the speaker simultaneously drops his or her voice to a much lower pitch, relaxing the vocal cords and making a creaky sound – especially at the end of words.

Try it. Say the word 'opportunity' so it sounds like—opportuniteeee —dropping down on the eees. If you don't recognize it on the page, you can check out how it sounds by searching online for Vocal Fry. While young men also use vocal fry, we tend to recognize it more in young women who 'fry' a lot at the end of sentences.

Sighs

Sighing is the long exhalation of breath. Sometimes the sound of the sigh is just the exhalation of air. Sometimes the air is accompanied by an open vowel sound: aaaghhh, huuuhhh. Vary the sighs in length, pitch, amount of breath and the vocal sound accompanying it, and you can convey a wide range of emotions and attitudes. For example:

1. Sighing on a softly voiced vowel may convey depression.

2. Sighing on a loudly voiced vowel could be used to reveal pomposity.

3. You may have a character sigh to convey their irritable nature.

4. Sighs can be used to indicate a character's intolerance of what, to them, is another person's obvious inferior intellect.

Deep, Extended Inhalations

Taking in a deep, long breath before speaking can indicate a person who is ill and has difficulty breathing. It can also be used effectively to indicate a character's heavier body weight, as it was in one book I directed. The audiobook actor had already voiced a zillion minor male characters, and as he was reading, up popped another one. It was a very minor character, with only a few lines, and the actor hadn't prepped a voice for him. The only thing we knew from the text was that the gentleman had a position of some, but not great, authority. The actor was brilliant, but I thought I saw his eyes nearly roll back in his head at the thought of handling the zillionth and one minor male character.

So I quickly suggested a Character Key: this man was in his 50s, had a high-pitched voice and thought way more highly of himself than anyone else did. He was quite portly, and his extra weight made it a little difficult for him to breathe, so he took deep, extended inhalations. I also suggested a descending cadence that implied the character's impatience with his 'inferior' listeners. The actor added some deeps sighs during this character's dialogue to indicate that the 'mighty man' was waiting for his 'inferior' listener to catch up with his brilliance. The character was a minor one, but with that Character Key, he became so distinctive, and so much fun to portray, he became one of our favorites.

Delicate, Whispery Speech

Whispers are created when the vocal cords are rigid and don't vibrate, thus you only hear the sound of your breath moving past them. Add a soft vocal on top of that and you'll get whispery, delicate sounding speech.

1. You can use this pattern to indicate a non-threatening character.

2. You can use it to convey a character's spiritual sensibility. It's a voice often used on meditation tapes.

Accents

An accent is a combination of word pronunciation and cadence. While there may be general similarities between accents in a large regional area, like the American South for example, there can be distinct accent differences between groups in that region. If you're reading a character from Georgia, make sure you're not giving her an Alabama accent just because she's from the South. You don't want to stereotype an accent. What an author might refer to as an Italian-American accent would be different depending on whether, for example, your character was from Brooklyn or Boston or Italy.

An accent that is important to have in your arsenal is alternately referred to as Standard American English, General American English or Neutral English. It is considered to be American English spoken with no regionalisms. Of course, whatever a community's accent is, that's the standard, neutral, unaccented speech for that community.

For audiobook actors, unless a book is meant to be performed with a particular accent, you'll be expected to read it using Standard American English, so having it in your back pocket gives you a wider range of possibilities for casting. For a quick reference, listen to television newscasters. They use Standard American English.

Don't try to fake an accent. I've worked with actors who assured me of their accent proficiency, then showed up with a cliché version of the required accent. One actor was adamant that he could do a Jamaican accent, but his Jamaican sounded more like a general Irish accent. If you don't know how to do a particular accent, get help! And there are many resources for that help:

1. Check the internet for the proper pronunciation of words in the accent needed. You can find movies, shows, speakers of every language, dialect and accent. YouTube is where you'll likely find a resource for every accent. Forvo.com is a website where you'll find, as they write, "All the words in the world. Pronounced." And they are pronounced by native speakers. If you need to research foreign words, it's a great resource. International Dialects of English Archive (IDEA), www.dialectsarchive.com, provides "primary-source recordings of English-language dialects and accents as heard around the world." And they provide details regarding the age, ethnicity and location of the speakers. Audioeloquence.com is a website that offers: "Pronunciation, Dialect & Speech Resources for Audiobook Narrators."

2. Ask a speaker of the language to record the lines you need the accent for, so you can capture the proper pronunciation, cadence and melody.

Years ago, a producer called me and said, "Do you still have your Greek accent? If so, I've got a part for you as the wife of Omar Shariff's character in a mini-series, *Memories of Midnight*."

I'd played the role of The Woman in *Zorba* on Broadway and while my character never said a single word, she sang—with a Greek accent. "Oh sure," I told the producer. "No problem."

It had been many years since I'd done the show, but I figured if I could hear my dialogue read by someone with a real Greek accent, I could get it back.

At least I hoped I could.

So, I ran over to my local Three Guys Greek diner with pages of my dialogue, and one of the Guys agreed to read it while I recorded him. After a little practice, my accent was solid, at least for my lines.

I sent in my audition and happily booked the job. Off I flew to Zagreb, Croatia, where we were filming and my first day on the set, one of the producers began speaking to me—in Greek! I was thrilled that he thought I was Greek, but I had to confess I had absolutely no idea what he was saying.

As you work on developing Character Voices for a book, it's easy to forget how you voiced someone who had dialogue forty pages back, especially after you've voiced other characters of similar age and background. Like stage actors can have a prompter—an offstage person who can remind them of dialogue—and TV performers may have cue cards or a teleprompter scrolling their lines, you can create a Character Voice prompt—a Prompter Voice.

The Prompter Voice

This is a recorded bit of a character's dialogue, read in the voice you created for that character. You record the Prompter Voice during your rehearsal on a device you can later refer to. As I noted, it's very hard to keep a wide range of Character Voices in your head throughout a production. So once you nail a character's voice during rehearsal, record it. If as you're working, you forget that voice, check the Prompter Voice.

If you'll be recording the actual production in a professional studio, it's best to use a small recording device you can bring with you. If you're recording in your home studio, you can record the Prompter Voices on whatever device works best for you. To keep the Prompter Voices organized and easily retrievable, note where each is on your recording system next to the character's name on the Character List you've created for the audiobook.

Once you're recording the actual production, your Prompter Voices can be used to help you recall any character's voice before you record their first dialog.

The Prompter Voice does not become part of the production; it's there to jog your memory. During the production, you'll be marking, creating a Memory Location for each character's first bit of dialogue.

Marking/Memory Location

Mark the recording of each character's first dialogue on your recording program's timeline, creating what is called a Memory Location.

That marked dialogue now becomes your go-to Character Voice reference. You'll be able to quickly bring it up if needed later in the session. You may have recorded a marked Character Voice slightly differently than on your Prompter Voice, so it's best to go to that character's Memory Location to perfectly match the voice later in the session. (If you're working in a professional studio, the engineer will be marking the Character Voices. For further explanation of Marking and Memory Location see the Glossary).

You may be recording over several days, or as noted, you may have a character reappear after forty pages. Or more! If you goof and use different voices for the same character, it's not pretty, which is exactly what happened during one production I was directing. We were at the end of a long session. The actor was adamant that his voice for a particular character, who last had dialogue about seventy pages back and now had a lot of new dialogue was on the money. He was 100% sure he was giving that character the same voice.

I wasn't so sure, but this was in the reel-to-reel days. You couldn't just go to the memory location and double check the voice. You had to search back through the recording which took time. It had been a long day and the actor wanted to finish up and leave. He was so talented and so insistent that the Character Voice was the same, that I figured he must be right. But it gnawed at me so at the end of the session, I asked him to wait and had my engineer search for the character's earlier dialogue. The voices were not a match. They weren't even close! We had to re-record pages and pages of dialogue and insert each line into the previously recorded material. I never made that mistake again, no matter how talented or persuasive the actor.

More Character Voice Workouts

Develop a Character Voice for the individuals listed below based on the Character Key given for each, and read the next text, KNOW WHO YOU ARE, in each of those voices.

Use any combination of the vocal elements and speech patterns we've reviewed—whisper, elongate vowels and/or consonants, speed it up, slow it down, drawl, upspeak, drop your consonants or articulate them carefully. Try giving the five characters various ethnicities and accents even when none is mentioned. Create a Prompter Voice for each.

ELISE: 40s, an extremely smart, quick thinking, sophisticated businesswoman. She is sharp, focused and unrelenting in her opinions.

ALFRED: 30s, a pompous, semi-successful businessman, wants to be seen as a mover and shaker.

REESE: A gentle, elderly teacher who is physically frail, but wants to be respected.

CLARISSE: 24, has her own YouTube channel promoting makeup and clothing products. She likes to present herself as sexy, kittenish and is constantly shooting and posting videos of herself.

CLARENCE: 40, a Southern minister of a mega-church. He sees himself as the inspiring leader of his followers.

Text: KNOW WHO YOU ARE

Whatever path you choose, whatever road or highway you take, you've got to know who you are. Yes, of course, you've heard that before. But it's simple and true. You are your greatest resource. Don't second guess yourself. I see too many people out there worried about what everyone else thinks of them. Well, guess what? The people you are worried about, are worried about you! What you think of them! Don't let that insecurity drag you down. Know who you are. Use your strengths. Don't let anything stop you.

Now read the RAIN text below in the same five Character Voices. Read them in the same order as you read them for the KNOW WHO YOU ARE text. If you recall each voice exactly, great! If not, check your Prompter Voice for whichever Character Voice you need help with. It may be hard to recall voice 1 (Elise) after you've done the four others.

Text: RAIN

It was raining, no, it was pouring when I left the restaurant, and I was totally, unprepared for rain. I had no umbrella, no raincoat. Nothing. I think the weather reporter had just looked out the window while the sun was still shining and then made his report. "Sunny! Very sunny!"

Of course, I was drenched. And I had no time to change before I had to make a presentation before a very important group of people.

So I told myself what I've told you. Don't let anything stop you.

Let's try a completely different character. This individual is loaded with self-confidence, and you can have a lot of fun playing with the rhythms, accent and vocal quality of their speech depending on the Character Key you create. In fact, give this character two different

Character Keys and Character Voices, and read the text twice. Give each one a name if that helps you create their Character Key.

Text: ATTITUDE

He said he was gonna call me, but I'm like waiting and waiting and he never calls. So I go to the club and he's there, and he's dancin' with Anita. But I'm dressed in some hot jeans and my brand-new shirt with the ruffle around the top, and I know I'm lookin' really good which Anita definitely was not. That girl needs a makeover!

So I was ignoring him but of course he sees me and when the music stops, he just leaves Anita and comes over to me and starts lookin' me up and down, which don't get me wrong, he should have because of how good I look. But I was like, "Uh, uh, no way, put your eyes back where they belong."

He laughed but then Anita comes over and starts givin' me attitude, like I did something to her.

As if.

As if I even care.

He'll be callin' me tomorrow.

Definitely!

Possible Character Key: 20, Urban girl of any ethnicity, high energy, very self-confident.

Possible Character Voice: High pitched, rapid-fire delivery.

Alternate Character Key: 30, any gender, New Yorker, extremely judgmental and sarcastic.

Alternate Character Voice: Low and throaty, extends words for maximum effect, vocal fry.

In Mary Shelly's novel, *Frankenstein: or, the Modern Prometheus*, Robert Walton is writing to his sister of a strange occurrence while

Captain of a ship traveling to the North Pole. Use this excerpt to focus on reading with an accent. Walton is British. If you don't have a British accent in your arsenal, use any of the suggestions in the section on accents to see how you can 'cross the pond' on this one. With regard to his Character Key, Walton is twenty-eight when he begins his journey. Since he is the captain of a ship, you know he's courageous and knowledgeable. Given his age, those traits and that he is British, you can create a Character Voice for him. Read the letter as if it's dialogue, as if Robert is speaking (not writing) to his sister. Again, you don't have to have read the book for our purposes.

Text: LETTER IV (Excerpt)

To Mrs. Saville, England

August 5th, 17----

So strange an accident has happened to us that I cannot forbear recording it, although it is very probable that you will see me before these papers can come into your possession.

Last Monday (July 31st), we were nearly surrounded by ice, which closed in the ship on all sides, scarcely leaving her the sea-room in which she floated. Our situation was somewhat dangerous, especially as we were compassed round by a very thick fog. We accordingly lay to, hoping that some change would take place in the atmosphere and weather.

About two o'clock the mist cleared away, and we beheld, stretched out in every direction, vast and irregular plains of ice, which seemed to have no end. Some of my comrades groaned, and my own mind began to grow watchful with anxious thoughts, when a strange sight suddenly attracted our attention, and diverted our solicitude from our own situation. We perceived a low carriage, fixed on a sledge and drawn by dogs, pass on towards the north, at the distance of half a mile: a being which had the shape of man, but apparently of gigantic stature, sat in the sledge, and guided the dogs. We watched the rapid progress of the traveler with our telescopes, until he was lost.

Combining background, personality, accent and elements of speech should enable you to create a wide array of Character Voices. But sometimes, despite your best efforts, the perfect voice for a character eludes you. You're stuck.

Model the Character Voice

If you're having trouble giving a character their voice, think of someone you know whose personality is similar to that character and model the Character Voice after their voice. You don't need to copy the voice, rather let it inspire you. It doesn't even have to be a human. One actor used Eeyore, the donkey, a character from A.A. Milne's *The House at Pooh Corner*, as the model for a small-town sheriff in a book we did. Hey, if it works—and it did—why not?

Don't mimic or try to impersonate a well-known person's voice. A friend or family member can also serve as inspiration and reference for Character Voices. Any quirky or interesting personality trait reflected in their voice and speech pattern can become the basis of a great Character Voice. Your tough-as-nails dictatorial grandmother, that great uncle whose laughter comes out in little snorts between words, your playful kid sister with a squeaky sound who thinks everything is just 'soooo fun,' all can be modeled to create unique Character Voices. They might be thrilled to have their sound immortalized in an audiobook, unless you're modeling them for a really mean character. In that case, they'll never realize it was them.

Reading Another Gender

It's difficult to sound exactly like another gendered character. If you can do it, that's great and it can be a plus, but it isn't expected or necessary. Conveying their personality, their emotional approach to a situation or response to another character is what's important. When it comes to the vocal sound, men, when reading women, can soften their voice a bit and try to pitch it a little higher than the male characters in the book, but never to where it sounds silly or cartoonish. Women, when reading men, need to pitch their voices down a bit, but again, never to where it sounds phony. If you are voicing a non-binary identifying character, find a voice you think represents their self-identification.

Organizing Character Voices in An Audiobook Series

When you're recording a series, you may record a number of the audiobooks in quick succession, or there may be a long time between productions. Either way, memory can be a tricky thing, especially if you're doing a series with a great variety of characters, many of whom may be of the same background, gender, age, etc. For one series I produced and directed, the author wrote another book several years after we thought we'd completed the series. The new book featured numerous characters the actor had voiced years ago and would have to match now! There was no way he could remember the voice of one particular farmer he'd voiced years before in the first audiobook after having voiced about twenty other farmers of similar age with similar accents in subsequent productions.

The Executive Producer called me. "Do you," she asked hopefully, "still have samples of the Character Voices for the prior books?" Happily, I did. Because as we recorded the series, the engineer and I had created a Character List document and a Character Voice audio file—a dedicated computer file with a sample of each Character Voice in order of appearance for each of the prior books. And we'd saved them. Thus we had access to all the voices the actor had to match. For instructions on how to create, organize and correlate the Character List document and Character Voice audio file, see Appendix 1: Organizing Character Voices in an Audiobook Series.

Whether you are recording a series or one book, no matter who your characters are, how old they are, what their personalities, genders and voices are like, every one of them wants something. They've each got an objective in the story: love, redemption, revenge, success, fame, a new job. They may want to be honored, appreciated, to solve the mystery, to win the battle. The possibilities are endless.

If they didn't want something, they wouldn't be in the book.

11

Character Objectives

Don't be afraid to go out on a limb. That's where the fruit is.
—Arthur Lenehan

Overall Objective

The overall objective is what a character wants to achieve by the end of the story, e.g.: power, love, acclaim, to rescue a child, to catch the criminal, to redeem one's honor, to be of value.

All the characters in a story have an overall objective, and their objectives create the book's conflict and drama as everyone strives to get what they want.

Still, it's the main character's overall objective that drives the story, and sometimes discovering that, helps you identify a point of view and tone.

I was asked, on extremely short notice, to produce and direct the audiobook version of a novel, which, though fiction, was written as if it was the first-person autobiography of Micky Mantle, the Hall of Fame baseball player. The first session would begin the next morning. I asked an excellent actor I knew to narrate. Thankfully he said yes, although he had almost no time to prepare.

We received the script late that evening, and I read it through. It was to say the least, quite dirty! It appeared at first, to be written from the point of view of Mantle as an old man who was proud of his youthful, extremely gross sexual exploits. It seemed that his overall objective was *admiration* for his prowess off the field. The tone appeared to be *braggadocio*. While the book was well-written, the actor and I were so uncomfortable about the salacious material, we asked that our names not be used for the credits.

We began the session early the next morning, and the text quickly became low down and dirty. The engineer, a very young guy, was blushing and couldn't look at me. The actor tried reading a paragraph then stopped. He started again then stopped again. Finally, he said, "I cannot say these words in front of you."

That was sweet of him, but we had to get the recording done. I stopped the session to figure out how to proceed with a supremely embarrassed actor and engineer and limited time. I remembered that there was a point in the book where the Mantle character desired to make things right with his family and be forgiven.

That was it! That was the key to turning the production around.

The Mantle character's overall objective, I realized, was not *admiration* but *forgiveness*! He was hoping that by revealing every detail of his past excesses, he could expiate his sins and be forgiven.

With that new overall objective, the reading completely changed. The Mantle character was no longer seeing his own behavior from the point of view of *pride* but from the point of view of *shame and regret*. Based on the new overall objective and new point of view, the book's tone changed from *braggadocio* to *confessional*. The personality of the book narrator, the Mantle character, changed from a *callous braggart* to a *humbled person* needing redemption. Instead of reveling in ugly conquests and mistreatment of women, the reading now expressed embarrassment and humility and a longing for forgiveness. Now the actor could say the words he couldn't say before. We weren't changing the story, we were connecting to, and giving voice to the author's words and intent in a different way.

As I've noted earlier, the tone or point of view may be what you connect to in a story first. Another director and actor may have decided to change the tone. Another director and actor might have looked at the story from a different point of view. But in this case, it was changing the main character's overall objective that gave us the key to the story. And when that new overall objective was implemented, everything changed with it. The words were the same, but what a difference it brought to the meaning of the story, the emotion the actor could supply it with and the new facets of the Mantle character's personality he could bring to light

The human experience, in art as in life, is complex and fascinating, and so you have the opportunity to be an archaeologist of the soul.

The actor and I were both dreading the review of the production and were greatly surprised when it got a very good one. Too bad we hadn't used our names.

Overall Objective Workout

Let's return to THE TRIP (further expanded). What do you see as the main character's overall objective? Does identifying it and reading with that in mind change your performance or the original point of view and tone you gave the story?

Text: THE TRIP (further expanded)

I couldn't believe our luck. We'd slogged through thirty miles of muddy red earth for over five hours in a barely held together minibus, the pride of the local population. We were averaging an 'amazing' six miles an hour and shared the ride with two women carrying a goat that was baaing loudly, one woman carrying a baby that soon started wailing, and an old man who scolded the driver any time the bus slowed down.

And to top all of that, Armand and I had to get out and help dig the minibus out of a rut the size of Texas. Twice.

We had pretty much run out of water, just a few drops left per our two bottles, and Armand, crabby as ever, kept complaining that the heat was sucking the juice out of him. He is usually a guy who sees the glass as half empty. This time he was seeing it as totally empty. He was getting to be a downer.

Okay, even I wasn't sure our water would last long enough to get us into the village where we could hopefully buy a couple of bottles of water. Or at least soda. Every store sells some kind of soda.

Oh, and about the luck part? It's that we made it. We didn't drop of heat exhaustion or dehydration.

We'd been planning to stay in this village for about a week, find our long-lost buddy D'Arcy, chill for a bit and then find another way back to the town. But I immediately knew I'd have to stay here longer, get a feel of the place, and its wonderful assortment of people. Armand, though, decided to move on.

I'd taken a room in a little guest house. I'd been there a week when one night, at about 11 p.m., I left for dinner and was set on by three men and forced back to my room. They stole nearly everything. Money? Gone! Bags? Gone! Watch? Gone. Luckily, they let me keep the clothes I was wearing. Also, luckily, the bus driver that stopped at the village the next day agreed to haul me back to civilization, but at an increased price, adding a bit of interest, for his having trusted that I'd pay when we made it back to town.

Possible Objectives: The adventure of a lifetime, or an experience that means I've really lived, or accept a challenge that tests my mettle.

Scene Objectives

These are the intermediary goals a character sets in order to achieve his overall objective. In our production of the novel featuring the Micky Mantle character, for example, to obtain his overall objective of *forgiveness*, some of his scene objectives in our production were *to bare himself, to humble himself, to confess*.

Joe Morton's (*Scandal*, *God Friended Me*) extraordinary reading of *Invisible Man*, Ralph Ellison's classic novel, demonstrates the power of scene objectives. The nameless Black protagonist's overall objective was *authenticity*. He is sensitive, having been hurt all his life, and is, certainly at the beginning of the book, naïve. But he is seeking authenticity from those who can never see the real human being that he is. His blackness makes his humanity invisible to them. His scene objectives—*approval, a job, visibility, power* (and others)—are steps he believes will bring him closer to obtaining his overall objective. But the character's scene objectives are not fulfilled until finally, bereft of everything, he lives underground and becomes truly invisible to everyone but himself, and finally, there, achieves his overall objective of *authenticity*.

Of course, in order to achieve an objective, a character must do something.

12

Character Actions

Things do not happen. Things are made to happen.
—John F. Kennedy

An action is something we do to affect an outcome, to attain our objective. It can be a physical action: we *run* to win a race, we *reach* for an object, we *hug* a child. It can be an emotional one: we *charm*, we *pressure*, we *cajole*. An action is always a verb; it is what we do, not what we feel. A character may feel desperate to get home so he *races* to catch that last train to his station. A character may feel attracted to someone, so she *flirts* or *teases* to obtain her objective—that person's attention. Another character may feel angry at someone, so their action might be to *castigate, come down on,* or maybe *sneer at* to try to obtain their objective—*an apology*.

A character's actions will often be described in the book's narrative but where you get to put emotional actions into full force is in the dialogue.

The emotional actions you give the characters, will be influenced by their Character Keys as expressed in their Character Voices, including the vocal attributes you give them. A confident, aggressive person at a high stakes job interview may use a different action to attain their objective—the job—than would an insecure person, or someone with an inflated ego. The outgoing, confident person, who speaks smoothly, with no hesitations, might *command* the situation. An insecure person, whose speech pattern is breathy, with many hesitations, might *cautiously appeal*. An ego-head who speaks loudly, stretching some words for perceived effect, might *grandstand*. The more specific the emotional actions you choose for a character in their dialogue, the more dimension you give that character, and the more believable and impactful their dialogue will be.

Character Actions Workouts

For this workout, let's go back to the recordings of the Character Voices you developed for:

ELISE: 40s, an extremely smart, quick thinking, sophisticated businesswoman. She is sharp, focused and unrelenting in her opinions.

ALFRED: 30s, a pompous, semi-successful businessman, wants to be seen as a mover and shaker.

REESE: A gentle, elderly teacher who is physically frail, but wants to be respected.

CLARISE: 24, has her own YouTube channel promoting makeup and clothing products. She likes to present herself as sexy, kittenish and is constantly shooting and posting videos of herself.

CLARENCE: 40, a Southern minister of a mega-church. He sees himself as the inspiring leader of his followers.

Read the following text in each of the five Character Voices you developed, making sure you match the voice you originally created for each character. Give the characters the same objective: *to not be arrested*. Give each an action appropriate for their Character Key as each one tries to avoid being jailed for breaking and entering.

Text: LET ME EXPLAIN

"Officer, please, if you'll let me explain. I'd been out on what I had thought would be a leisurely walk through the woods but suddenly, as if from nowhere, a storm rolled in. The thunder sounded like explosions. I ran as quickly as I could towards a house on the edge of the woods and as soon as I reached it, I hurried up the front steps and rang the doorbell but no one answered. I knocked, but no lights came on. The rain was pelting me and lightning was stabbing the sky constantly and getting real close. I had to get inside. I tried the door and it was open so I went in. I never touched a thing; I was just trying to avoid being out in a deadly situation. I guess I was exhausted or something and…and… well, I just fell asleep. I know I must have frightened the family when they returned but…you can see… I didn't mean any harm."

When determining the actions that characters take in pursuit of their objectives, the text of the story will give you a good deal of information that can help you make your choices, but always keep the Character Key in mind. Even if the above workout had included narrative that described, for example, the character being fearful and pleading, the pompous businessman would plead quite differently than might Clarisse, the YouTuber, who might be trying to impress her fans as she videos herself and the officer.

The text of the story can also guide your choice of actions by the attributives the author uses. Attributives are the words that identify who is speaking: the 'he saids,' and 'she saids' the writer uses. But attributives can be more than just speaker identifiers; they can simultaneously identify the action the character uses in her dialogue. If the text says she *fumed*, or she *sneered*, she *raged* or she *whispered alluringly*, the writer has told you exactly what action the character is using at that moment. And it will likely work for the rest of the scene unless the writer changes the attributive.

You need to read the dialogue using the action indicated by the attributive. You can't *sneer* when the text says he *laughed*, or *laugh* when it says he *fumed*. If the text says he *fumed*, you've got to fume. You might fume subtly or fume passionately; your fuming might be tightly wound or bursting forth, but fume you must, or it will sound like you've made an error.

Attributives are read in the book narrator's voice, which will most often be your natural voice, so you'll be switching back and forth between that and a Character Voice. It's easy to slip up and read the attributives in the voice of the character who is speaking, but after some practice it will become easier and easier to make the switches.

Following is the LET ME EXPLAIN TEXT with a few attributives added in. Choose one of the Character Voices you recorded reading this text previously, but this time you'll read it switching between the Character Voice and your own voice when reading the attributives.

For this reading I've noted the attributive pronouns as s(he). Use the appropriate pronoun for the character you're voicing. Give the character the same objective as you did in the prior reading: *to not be arrested*. You may use the same action(s) as you originally did, but if reading with the attributives leads you to different actions, use the new ones.

Text: LET ME EXPLAIN (with attributives)

"Officer, please, if you'll let me explain," s(he) said breathing heavily, "I'd been out on what I had thought would be a leisurely walk through the woods but suddenly, as if from nowhere, a storm rolled in. The thunder sounded like explosions," s(he) implored. "I ran as quickly as I could towards a house on the edge of the woods and as soon as I reached it, I hurried up the front steps and rang the doorbell but no one answered. I knocked," s(he) asserted forcefully, "but no lights came on. The rain was pelting me, and lightning was stabbing the sky constantly and getting real close. I had to get inside. I tried the door and it was open so I went in. I never touched a thing; I was just trying to avoid being out in a deadly situation." S(he) smiled for a moment and her/his voice became gentler. "I guess I was exhausted or something and...and... well," s(he) confessed, "I just fell asleep. I know I must have frightened the family when they returned but..." s(he) said apologetically, "you can see... I didn't mean any harm."

In the above workouts, you've developed objectives and actions for a single character in monologue. But your characters will most often be talking to one another, in dialogue, and they should sound like they are responding to each other.

13

Multi-Character Dialogue

The only reason why we ask other people how their weekend was is so we can tell them about our own weekend.

—Chuck Palahniuk

Unless it's a multi-cast production, you will be playing all the characters, giving each one their Character Voice, so you've got to create believable interaction between them by yourself. Give each character their objective and actions. Then allow them to talk and respond to each other. Creating responsiveness between characters – meaning we hear them reacting to what the other character is saying and the way he is saying it—is key to creating believable dialogue. We've all had conversations in our heads. Now, you'll just be doing it out loud.

As with the narrative sections, dialogue does not have to be big to be effective. Even when a character's action is to fume or rage, you don't have to raise your voice. You don't have to yell or shout to convey that they are fuming or raging. You can convey that you're raging even if you whisper. You're not onstage trying to reach a large audience, you're in the ears of one person at a time, or you're coming through a car audio system. If you need to practice big, fine. Just bring it down when recording.

Dialogue Workouts

Here's an extended version of the text THE BOXER that you worked on previously.

You've given the story a point of view and tone. You've set it in its culture and can give the narrative experiential immediacy. Now, give the boxer, his coach, and the assistant coach, their Character Keys, Character Voices and their overall objectives and action(s) for their dialogue.

What comes up for you as the boxer's overall objective? Is it to just get through the fight, or is it to be victorious? Is it to have a feeling of self-worth or perhaps to experience one moment of glory? Is it to gain his coach's respect?

What is the coach's overall objective? Is he seeking another victory for his coaching stats? Or is his objective to change his young boxer's self-perception? Is it to prove that he's still got the chops to develop a winner?

The assistant coach, though a minor character with only line, has an overall objective too. What do you see that as?

What action(s) do these people use to try to achieve their overall objectives?

The story is in first person, so the book narrator's Character Voice is the same as the Boxer's. However, you get to voice the Coach too, so this is a chance to explore your bad-ass, foul mouthed, cigar chomping inner warrior.

Text: THE BOXER (expanded)

Finally, I hear that damn bell ring. I'm six minutes into the first boxing match of my life at the 1977 N.J. golden gloves tournament. My opponent is confused. He doesn't know what to do with this six-foot three, one hundred and forty pound seventeen-year-old stick figure dancing in front of him. I have a pretty good left jab and so far it's kept him at bay, but it's just a ruse. I'm weak, and once he gets past my jab, I'll be helpless. And all the running around the ring it takes to keep him away from me is exhausting. My muscles are beginning to fail me.

If he pours it on, he'll run me over for sure. I don't think I can keep this charade up for another three minutes.

A thick cloud of bluish smoke hangs suspended in the huge armory where this event is taking place. It's coming mostly from the pimped out old men in the crowd all decked out in their purple suits and wide brimmed hats, smoking cigars and betting on the outcome of each fight – putting money down on the empty chairs between them as if they're in Vegas. I go to my corner and fall onto the stool waiting for me, sweat drenching my hair and my boxing trunks, the cigar smoke scorching my lungs, making me breathe like I'm having an asthma attack.

My coach, who goes by the nickname Tex, jumps in front of me and squirts water into my gaping mouth. A former world-class boxer, now in his sixties, Tex is the archetype of a fighter. He has no cartilage left in his nose to speak of. His eyes are mere slits from the years of scar tissue build-up. His is a face one is not born with; it is a face that is earned. It is a face that's a source of pride and respect in the fighting world.

"You're doing beautiful," he says, his gravelly voice and wise-guy accent exposing his past as a Newark street-tough. Tex hands the water bottle to the assistant coach who looks up at him and blurts out, "I think he's actually winning this fight!" Tex gives a subtle nod, obviously annoyed by the assistant's surprised tone. But I know why he's surprised. I am the least talented boxer on our team.

I have won a place in my coach's heart because I try so hard, but I am the weak link on this boxing squad. That's why Tex is not as tough on me as he is on the other members of the team. He is always careful not to jolt my fragile confidence in myself. During training I am constantly putting myself down and Tex is constantly building me up. He is more like a life coach than a boxing coach where I am concerned. I am coddled, and I know it.

"Just stick and move and you've got this one,"Tex encourages. Gasping for breath, I say, "I don't think I can keep this up another three minutes."

"Sure you can," he pushes back. "We've trained to go hard for nine minutes and that's what we're going to do."

"I can't. I can't," I say softly, dropping my head. Suddenly I feel a hard slap across my face, the sharp sound silencing the loud clamor of the crowd. I look up to see my coach's angry face three inches from mine. "Play time is over!" he roars. "Where the hell do you think you are!? And who the hell do you think I am!? You're not in the gym; you're at the God damned golden gloves! And let's get something clear. I'm not your fucking shrink, and you're not in a God damned head doctor's office where you can play your 'please make me feel good about myself' game!"

He steps aside and points to my opponent in the opposite corner.

"Look at him," he fumes. "He doesn't think he's in a fucking therapy session. He thinks he's in a fucking fight! I gave you the chance to fight that you wanted and you're not going to make me or this squad look like a bunch of candy-asses because you want to play this 'I'm not worthy' bullshit game! I've trained you to go nine hard minutes and you're going to give me nine hard minutes! Understood!?"

"Yes sir," I say, my breath suddenly calm. It takes a few seconds for his anger to dissipate. With a controlled, measured calmness he says, "Now you keep that left jab in his face and don't drop it on the way back. You're begging to be hit with a right. Get off first and don't let him inside. That's where he has the advantage. You got that?" he says.

"Got it!" I say back crisply. I stand up and Tex jumps out of the ring, dragging the stool with him. The third round is about to start. I take one last look at Tex leaning on the ring apron.

My eyes lock on to his. He yells up to me, "You're not an ordinary man, don't act like one! You're a warrior, act like what you are!" The bell rings, but what happens next is not important to me anymore. For this brief period, I am not the least on the team. I am not the coddled one. For this snapshot in time, I am a fighter! I am a warrior! And I have already won.[1]

Place/Period: Tough City Gym, 1970s

THE BOXER:

    Possible Character Key: 17, courageous, but insecure.

    Possible Character Voice: Mid-range, out of breath at times.

    Possible Objective: Self-respect, or a moment of glory, or his coach's approval.

    Possible Actions: Hang in, hold on, rise up.

THE COACH (TEX):

    Possible Character Key: 60s, from Newark, called Tex, rough, gritty, no-nonsense guy.

    Possible Character Voice: Low pitched, gravelly, gruff, punches out his words.

    Possible Objective: The Boxer's belief in himself, or that he himself is still a great coach.

    Possible Actions: Encourage, rip into, inspire.

THE ASSISTANT COACH:

    Possible Character Key: 50s, failed boxer, deferential.

    Possible Character Voice: Breathy, higher pitched than Coach.

    Possible Objective: The Coach's approval.

    Possible Actions: Encourage.

---

[1] Text THE BOXER by Neil Mitchell.

Let's return to High School Assistant Principal AP GO. In this scene, she is having a conversation with substitute teacher Phillip Lachman. He's very serious about, and committed to, teaching. She is very political, willing to bend the rules. For this reading, assume the book's tone is *deadpan humor* and the point of view is *irreverent*. Give each character their Character Key and Character Voice. Give each an overall objective and action(s) and let them duke it out as each one tries to get what he or she wants.

And here's that reminder to help you dig in:

> Read Aloud
>   Slow it Down
>   Do Nothing
>   Note it
>   Welcome the Unexpected
>   Don't Overdo it
>   Read as if to Someone You Know

Text: AP GO

I exited the bus along with several students, and as I walked into the Main Office, AP Go motioned me toward her office. She asked me to shut the door and sit down. I did.

"You look gray," she said. As always, she looked like a hot cheerleader. "Beg pardon?"

"Your skin. It looks gray. Are you sick?"

"I'm fine."

"Whatever you've got, I hope it's not contagious." The phone rang. She stared at it. Two, three, four rings.

She flipped her ponytail from one shoulder to the other. "It's never good. Never, ever good." Then she picked it up, and I studied my feet as she snappily assured the caller that she couldn't fire Mr. Morton for continually referring to a boy named Arash as Osama. But she'd talk with him ASAP and call back. She placed the phone in its cradle and eyeballed me. "Phyllis Shul, Nick's mom, complained about you. Want to tell me about it?"

"What'd she say?"

"I think you know."

"I don't."

"Nick is being recruited by Princeton to play tennis, or so she says. And it seems you've already sent him to detention for his tardies. Anything but As and Es on his five-week report card will destroy his chance for a scholarship. She's unhappy and when the co-chair of our annual Casino Night fundraiser is unhappy, I'm unhappy. So?"

"Nick Shul's been tardy every day. Three tardies and I give an S, eight or more, it's a U. And that's what I explained the first day of class. To everyone."

Go tapped her long red nails on her desk and glared at me. "Phyllis says Nick wasn't aware of any policy."

"That's because he's fifteen minutes late every morning. He missed the discussion on absences and tardies, but he was given a copy of the class rules."

"And you're not going to cut an AP student any slack? At the start of school?"

"He lives around the corner."

Go studied her thumbnail that seemed to have been filed to resemble a dagger. "Unacceptable," she said, shaking her head, sending the ponytail flying. "His mother said that if you won't be flexible on this, she'll want to meet with the two of us soon. Think about it, Mr. Lachman. As you know, my time is precious."

I'd had enough. I stood up. "If Nick can mosey into class fifteen minutes late, why not allow my students to show up twenty, thirty or sixty minutes late? Heck, why bother to come to first period at all?"

Assistant Principal Go stood and faced me, and though she was nearly a foot shorter, she looked tall and terrifying. "Mr. Lachman, whatever's going on in your life seems to be clouding your judgment and you're taking it out on one of our best students. Take some time, think it through. Flexibility is the key. I'm sure Mrs. Shul will be back in touch." She dismissed me with one last flip of her hair.[1]

AP GO:

Possible Character Key: 30s, American-Korean descent, no accent, tough, mean spirited.

Possible Character Voice: Higher pitched, terse, speaks with tight precision, clips her words.

Possible Scene Objective: Total control.

Possible Actions: Stab, degrade.

PHILLIP LACHMAN:

Possible Character Key: 39, loves teaching, smart, very funny, urban, acerbic wit, very moral.

Possible Character Voice: Lower register, languid, open vowels, slight New York accent.

Possible Scene Objective: Moral victory.

Possible Actions: Defend, confront.

Did the character's objectives stay the same or change as you read? Did you give each character one action, or did you find yourself changing actions in reaction to the other person's dialogue as the scene went on? Perhaps in your reading, AP Go began by *bossing* and wound up *degrading*. Perhaps substitute teacher Phillip started by *reasoning* and ended up *confronting*. Whatever your choices, were you able to keep the characters responding to each other? If not, a little practice will get you in the rhythm of the dialogue exchange.

---

[1] Dennis Danziger, *A Short History of a Tall Jew*. Deal Street Press, 2010.

In the following selection create three Character Voices. Keep in mind that Sharon is drunk, and a drunk person is usually trying to speak as if they are not drunk. Let her slur, elongate, stammer, pause, rush, do whatever you come up with to convey her inebriated state. See where the scene takes you, how much fun you can have with their dialogue as you give these characters objectives and actions. If switching between the three characters' dialogue, the attributives and the narrative is difficult at first, read each character's lines separately. (If needed, you can do that when you're recording in the studio; editing can make it sound seamless.) Notice how some of the attributives let you know what the character's action is. For example, when you read "Mercy urged," in the text, the attribution clearly lets you know that her action there is to urge.

Text: SHARON AND MERCY

The music was country, and the bar was pretty packed. It was after midnight and Sharon's friend Mercy was trying to get her to slow down on the drinking.

"I think we should pack it up for the night," Mercy urged.

"Nuh uh," Sharon protested. "I may not be...as young as I used to beee...but I can shtill handle my liquor....uh...like I'm a...a...teenager!" As she got to the end of the sentence, she began to tilt backwards.

"Whoopsie," she laughed.

"I'm serious," Mercy said, reaching out to steady her. "We have to be at work tomorrow Let's go."

"No way," Sharon laughed as she brought her glass up to her lips. "You don't foooool me. Tomorrow...is...hmmm..oh! It's Shaturday! And you are killing the vibe! Ha ha!!!! You're dragging me down."

"Oh honey," the bartender, who was ready with the bottle, cooed as he offered Sharon a refill. "You need another taste?"

"Tomorrow is Friday." Mercy snapped, prying Sharon's glass from her hand. "It's not 'Shaturday' and thank you," she said, glaring at the bartender, "but she obviously doesn't need a taste."

"The name's Evan," he laughed, "I've seen her here a few times and she never refuses another taste."

"Seeee?" Sharon giggled. "Evan knows me best. You are Evan, right?

"You are right honey."

"No more honey tonight," Mercy said, "I'll be dragging you out if you don't start walking. Give me your car keys."

"Noooo."

"Now!" Mercy demanded.

"You are a true friend," Sharon mumbled, digging in her purse. "Boring, but true."

SHARON:

Possible Character Key: 30s, fun loving, irresponsible.

Possible Character Voice: Light, pitched high,
    rising/falling cadence.

Possible Objective: Fun, to get blasted.

Possible Actions: To revel, whoop it up.

MERCY:

Possible Character Key: 30s, restrained, reliable.

Possible Character Voice: Low voice, slightly nasal,
    sharp pattern.

Possible Objective: Get Mercy home safely.

Possible Actions: Urge, pressure.

EVAN:

Possible Character Key: 30s, knows the ropes,
    good sense of humor.

Possible Character Voice: Deep and throaty.

Possible Objective: A big tip.

Possible Actions: Encourage, flirt.

No ethnicities are given for Sharon, Mercy and Evan. Give them any ethnicities you like. Try different ones.

In the next selection, PHIL AND JIMMY G. are two cops who come from different worlds. They're having an easy-going conversation, but even when people are just casually shooting the breeze, both parties want something. It can be as simple as *comradery, to establish a bond, to get respect, to impress,* or *to have fun.* It can be to *assess trust,* or whatever else you come up with. Give them each a Character Key, Character Voice, objectives and actions.

Text: PHIL AND JIMMY G.

Jimmy G. slid into the front seat of the car next to Phil. They were heading downtown to a farewell send-off for one of the detectives who was retiring. Jimmy was fairly new to the department, a twenty-four-year-old who lived in Brooklyn and was pumped to be working in Manhattan. Phil had been a detective for about twenty years now, and he knew Jimmy G. was aiming to make detective too. He thought he was a smart kid who brought a good energy to the squad, but Phil also thought he was a little too inflexible, not that it was his business, but Phil made everything his business.

Phil started driving and turned the radio to a rock station. His head was nodding side to side with the beat as they pulled onto the FDR going south.

Jimmy listened to the music for a minute then shook his head.

"Man, that is old school!" he said. "Where'd you find that station?"

"You like it?" Phil asked.

"You kiddin' me? No offense, but this stuff went out with the dinosaurs."

"Hey. This is 104 point three. New York's finest Classic Rock station. These bands are legendary. Gods of Rock!" Phil said in his gravelly voice. "Have a little respect."

"Sorry," Jimmy said, "but I like the new stuff. I'm not down with this."

"Well, millions of people are. You ever really check it out?"

"Nah. Not interested."

"You wanna change the station?" Phil said. "No problem."

"You sure man? It'll be a big change for you. You may not be able to take it."

"Hey, I can take it. I embrace change."

"You? No disrespect," Jimmy laughed, "but isn't that the same crew cut you got in high school?"

"Different barber."

"And you're famous for having the same lunch every day. Turkey on rye and a Cel-Ray soda."

"People talk about my lunch?"

"Oh yeah. Cel-Ray soda? Definitely old school. Everybody knows that and everybody knows that you do not change."

"Hey, sometimes I go for Pastrami and a Coke, but that's not the change I'm talking about. I was thinking about ideas. I'm open to new ideas."

"I got plenty of ideas," Jimmy said.

"Yeah, but I'm talking in philosophical terms. See, the question is, can you adapt your ideas? Not necessarily change, but adapt as change comes for you, confronts you."

"Change that comes for you?" Jimmy said thoughtfully. "That's deep."

Jimmy liked that idea, the way Phil put it: that change seeks you out, that it finds you. It's what he was hoping for. That he could move up and that he could handle the challenges in good way.

"You want to make detective someday, right Jimmy?" Phil suddenly said, breaking into Jimmy's thought.

"Definitely. Narcotics. Undercover maybe."

"Then you gotta be fast thinking for sure. Your neurons got to be fired up."

"My neurons are plenty fired," Jimmy laughed. "Maybe it's been a while since you needed those fired up neurons, but don't worry about mine. They are locked and loaded. In a manner of speaking."

Phil laughed, then pushed a button on the radio, turned up the volume and suddenly, a hip hop station blasted on.

"See?" he said to Jimmy. "I had it programmed. That's change comin' atcha. Unexpected right? You gotta be open to the unexpected. And I still got some unexpected left in me."

"Well you better get some neurons to be working too bro." Jimmy laughed. "You just missed our exit!"

"Damn!!!" Phil exclaimed.

Jimmy laughed again. "Stay tight man, it's just a little change."

At this point, you know what to do. So from the PHIL AND JIMMY G. story on, the Possibles that have been placed at the end of Texts, will be found in Appendix 2: The Possibles, to be used if you need them.

Let's return to THE EXISTENTIAL COWBOY. When we left Mike and his girlfriend Suzy, they'd followed two cowboys into the Dew Drop Inn. Use the point of view and tone you've given the story. Use the descriptions written in the story to create Character Keys and Character Voices. Give the characters their objectives and actions, and let them talk to each other.

Text: THE EXISTENTIAL COWBOY (continued)

Mike and Suzy sat down at the bar; the heavier cowboy closest to them. In the most richly Darth Vaderesque voice, the man introduced himself as "Monte." The skinnier one leaned across. "Name's Tom," he said. "And I'm just wondering what the hell y'all are doing here. You look more out of place than a nudist at a wedding!" Suzy giggled at that while Mike smiled slightly.

"This is Suzy, guys, and I'm Mike," he said, extending his hand. He paused for a second wondering how open to be with these strangers. It was apparent that they'd been sitting at the bar for a while now. The bartender approached. Seeing as how the cowboys were drinking beer, Mike and Suzy ordered the same.

What the hell, Mike thought. Maybe these guys are too wasted to laugh at me. He cleared his throat. "Ever since I was a little boy," he began, "I wanted to be a cowboy and that's why we're here. I'm looking for a place to buy." Before he would look at their faces for a reaction, he plunged a couple of fingers into the nut bowl the bartender had scooted in front of them when they ordered their drinks, pulled out a few and, in a cupped hand, rushed them to his mouth.

"What do you know about ranchin' and raising cattle?" the voice from the deep Darth Vader well asked, his head cocked to one side while looking straight at Mike's munching mouth. Mike was again drawn up by the man's huge, deep sonorous voice; a voice that could have rattled the glasses on the bar. Definitely someone out of a John Ford Western, he thought. He wondered if Monte could sing. He swallowed the bar nuts. "Would you mind telling me if you've ever sung or done any TV commercials? You've got that kind of voice." Monte winked, smiled, swayed on the stool a bit, and whispered, "I once was an extra in a John Ford movie!"

Mike roared. "Just what I was imagining! And in answer to your question about ranching, I know nothing, just what I've seen in the movies and on TV." Monte turned to his friend and in a ridiculous attempt at a whisper—more like the voice of God bellowing a car commercial, said something that sounded like "cue," and "night" and "Clint." Tom whispered back. Suzy, with a look of skepticism, wondered nervously what plan these two inebriates were hatching.

Monte then swiveled around and boomed, "How would you city slickers like to visit a real cattle ranch operation? We're having a BBQ at our spread this evening and you're more than welcome to drop by." Susy giggled again, Mike smiled, stuck out his hand and said, "What time?"

They returned to the Jockey Club and got ready for the festivities. In a moment of "what the hell" abandon, Mike had bought himself a pair of custom Lucchese cowboy boots made in Texas. They were dark brown with a hand-tooled floral design and a three-inch heel. He'd put them on and imagine he was Gary Cooper on the dusty streets of *High Noon*.

"My God," Suzy said. "You'll never fit in the car with those boots on!"

"I'll put the top down and climb over the door!" he laughed. Mike grabbed her around the waist and led her to the full-length mirror behind the bedroom door. "Look at us," he said. "A regular Roy Rogers and Dale Evans!" Suzy looked at him in the mirror, puzzled, too young to remember the iconic cowboy couple of Mike's youth. "Never mind," he laughed. "Let's go."[1]

When working on a story with many different characters who have dialogue, it can sometimes get confusing as to which character is speaking next. Color Coding is a tool that can help in that situation.

---

[1] Text THE EXISTENTIAL COWBOY by Ira Marks.

Color Coding

Assign a particular color to each character, and highlight or underline the character's dialogue in that color. This can help you quickly identify which character is speaking and which one will be speaking next. Just don't forget who's got which color.

We've focused on adult voices and conversation, but there are a great number of wonderful books featuring kids of all ages.

14

Character Voices For Children, Middle Grade (Tweens), and Young Adults (YA)

The real menace in dealing with a five-year-old is that in no time at all you begin to sound like a five-year-old.
—Jean Kerr

If you can sound like a five-year old, a ten-year-old or a fifteen-year-old that's good news. Children's, Middle Grade, and Young Adult (YA) audiobooks are very popular. These books are well written, with strong insight into character. They often take on complex and emotionally challenging situations: love, death, divorce, racism, drug abuse, illness, etc., yet reflect the reading level, the emotional interests, and maturity of the book's target age group.

Reading accuracy is particularly important for children's audiobooks. While a few very small errors that don't change the meaning of the text may be acceptable in adult literature (for example saying "they hurried" rather than "they all hurried"), errors are not acceptable in children's audiobooks. That's because audiobooks are often used as an adjunct to reading instruction, so it is extremely important that the words children hear match the words they see on the page. You'll have an opportunity to fix any word errors you make in a production, but you want to be as accurate as possible in your reading.

For all the different age groups you can use many of the vocal elements described for adult voices.

Young Children: 4-7

Character Key

There are no generic kids. While their voices may often sound similar, they are still individuals; some are shy, some are gentle and sweet, others are insecure, and others are full of bravado. Because their personalities are not yet complex, the young child's Character Key can be as simple as:

BRIANNA: 5, spunky, bouncy personality.

JUAN: 6, sensitive, shy.

JULANI: 5, very brave and gung-ho.

JAMMAL: 4, funny, likes to be silly.

Character Voice

Use the vocal elements reviewed, and remember, not all little kids have high pitched voices, some have lower throaty ones. Little kids are often speaking while working out what they're going to say, in which case they rush some words out, pause...then slow down as they gather their thoughts for the rest of the sentence. That creates an interesting speech pattern you can use. They can be very expressive, sharing their excitement with laughs and giggles. Shy kids might speak quietly and whispery, while bold kids often speak loudly and quickly to ensure you are paying attention to them.

Character Voice: Young Children Workouts

The following text features a young child telling their grandmother about their upcoming birthday party. Using the Character Keys for Brianna, Juan, Julani, and Jammal, give each child a Character Voice and read the following text, MY BIRTHDAY PARTY, in each child's voice.

Text: MY BIRTHDAY PARTY

My birthday party is going to be so fun grandma. We are going to play a lot of games, and I..I..I think I'm going to win them. Like the piñata. I like that 'cause it's fun. You hit the donkey and lots of candy falls all over the floor. And I'm gonna get presents and...then we eat cake and everybody sings "Happy Birthday" to me.

The following text features three-year olds Nia, Brian, Hilda, and Nia's mother. Create a Character Key and Character Voice for each based on the information the text provides.

Text: WHAT DID YOU DO TODAY

"What did you and Brian and Hilda do in school today?" Nia's mother asked as the children sat down for a snack. Nia was three years old now. She and Brian and Hilda were in the same class and they always played together after school. "I... umm... I made a big A with crayons," Nia said happily, waving her hands around. "Then we...we...went out...to...play. And," she giggled, "Brian picked his nose."

"Did not," Brian said defensively. "I never pick my nose." But Brian's nose was so stuffy it sounded like he said, "I dever bick by dose."

"I don't pick my nose either," Hilda said in her soft voice. "Can I have a carrot?"

Middle Grade (Tweens): 8-12

Character Key

Kids this age are in transition, eager for independence but still attached to parents. They're discovering more about themselves and are very influenced by friends, advertising, and older kids. Their personalities are becoming more complex.

Character Voice

As boys hit puberty their voices start to crack and get significantly lower. Girls' voices begin to change at that time as well. These kids are maturing, but they are still innocent, which gives them a more direct, less nuanced speech pattern than adults. Still, you can give them most of the vocal elements you've explored for adults: speed of speech, huskiness, breathiness, nasality, vocal fry, etc. You can get a good feel for their voices and speech patterns by listening to tweens as they're talking and interacting with their peers or adults. And a few kid movies can help if you aren't around any tweens.

Character Voice: Middle Grade (Tweens) Workouts

In this selection, Emma, Jenny and Marla are all approaching twelve-and-a-half, live in New Jersey and are middle school best friends. Emma is smart and loves writing, especially her secret poetry which she shows no one. She has a major crush on Aaron, the lead singer of her favorite band, Boyz3000. Jenny, her number two BFF, has a crush on a different member of the band. Emma and Jenny are in conversation, but Emma recalls her number one BFF Marla's dialogue. Give all the girls simple Character Keys and Character Voices. Even though Emma is repeating what Marla has said, give Marla a Character Voice too. Give all the girls objectives and actions. These can be very simple, appropriate for tween girls. And of course, give the story a tone and point of view.

Text: EMMA

Only my number two BFF Jenny knows about my feelings for Aaron. Jenny is very nice and perky, and she is a supportive person, so I felt okay telling her.

"You know Aaron? In Boyz3000?" I said. "Okay, so... don't tell anybody, but I like him. I mean I REALLY, REALLY like him!"

"He is totally adorable!!!" she squealed.

"Do you like him too?"

"No!!!! I mean yes, I like him, but not that way. I love Cory, their bass player. He is so cute."

"He is," I agreed, even though I hardly ever look at him on the posters.

"He's awesome," she said, sighing. "Totally awesome."

I was very relieved that we don't like the same boy. And kind of glad I could tell her about it. I tried to talk to my number one BFF, Marla, about my feelings once, but she got all scientific. Marla is a science geek. I mean, she's normal and likes clothes and music and all, but she totally loves experiments with slime mold in a Petri dish, and analyzing the number of frogs disappearing in ponds. And she loves statistics.

"You know that thousands of girls like Aaron," she said. "Right?"

"So??" I said.

"So, it's statistically almost impossible that a pop star boy will date a fan." I should have known she'd say something like that.

"I mean, really," Marla went on. "You have to look at the odds. You can't just spend your life looking at a poster. I think it's stopping you from maybe liking a real boy."

I wanted to say, "Okay, just forget it."

But instead I said, "Whatever! I mean I just love his singing and his writing. That's all."

But that's not all. How do you change what you feel just because some stupid statistic says you don't have a chance?[1]

The following selection, also from *Emma G. Loves Boyz, A True Love Journal*, features a conversion between Emma and Josh, a cute boy she met in the Bahamas where she got to see a concert featuring Boyz3000. She's now got a big crush on Josh who is visiting her for the first time since they've gotten back. It's Emma's first date! Josh is also twelve and very into music. He's a cool boy, but sensitive. He lives in Brooklyn and likes Emma because she's smart and funny and, he discovers, her secret writing is good! The description of Josh gives you his Character Key. Based on that, give him his Character Voice and give both kids objectives and actions. Make sure the characters respond to each other in the dialogue as their emotions change during the scene.

Text: EMMA AND JOSH

He sat down and didn't say anything. I got us some sodas and chips because really, I couldn't think of anything to say either.

At first, we just chewed chips. My chewing sounded loud to me, like a big, huge crunch – crunch – crunch, even though I was only taking tiny bites of the chips so I wouldn't get Dianna's sweater messed up.

We were both still quiet, so I thought, Thiiiiiink of something to say!! Thiiiiiiink!!!! And I thought of something.

"How was the flight home?" I asked.

"It was okay," he said. "Yours?"

"Being thirty thousand miles above the earth and knowing that you yourself are actually zooming across the ocean is pretty awesome."

He laughed.

"What?" I said.

---

[1] Text EMMA AND JOSH from *Emma G. Loves Boyz, A True Love Journal*, Taro Meyer, Red Sky Presents, 2015.

"You said, thirty thousand miles above the earth."

"Oh no!" I said and started laughing too. "I meant thirty thousand feet."

"That sounds better," he nodded, pretending to be very serious. "The air would be really thin at thirty thousand miles up."

"Very scientific," I said. "Oh, how'd you do on your paper, the one about gas?" He laughed again. "You mean the one about greenhouse gases?"

"Right!"

"I aced it."

We kept talking, and I told him about Marla and how she liked working with slime mold petri dishes. He loved that because he likes slime mold too! I told him about Ms. Pinkens not grading my Most Impressive essay. And then I told him about my very first, one and only, school food fight. That cracked him up. "I wish I could have seen it," he said.

"Everyone in the lunchroom took pictures."

Oh my god, I thought. DID I JUST SAY THAT???

AM I TOTALLY CRAZY????

Why did I tell him that????

WHY? WHY? WHY?

"I have to see those pictures!" he said. "Are they on Facebook?"

Oh no, I was thinking. Me and my big mouth.

Of course they were on Snapchat. And Instagram! Everyone in school had seen them! I was going to show them to him on my phone so they'd be small, but he said he wanted to see them on a bigger screen! On the computer!

UGH!!! He could see the computer was right there, so what could I do? He went over to the desk and sat down in front of it. I got a chair and sat to the side. He clicked the mouse and a document was open on the screen.

"What's this?" he said.

"What's what?" I asked and pulled my chair closer.

"This!"

He was looking at my poem!!! I had left it open!!! I tried to grab the mouse, but he wouldn't let go, and then he started reading it out loud.

"Who wrote this?" he said when he finished.

"Um…" I said. "Uh…" Then he looked at me, and I must have been blushing or something because my cheeks felt hot and he went, "Hey, did you write this?"

"Oh well, yeah," I said. "I was just like, you know, playing around and…"

"Wow," Josh said. "This is really cool."

"You think?" My heart jumped when he said that.

"Yeah. I do."

Young Adult (YA): 13-18

Character Key

Teens in Young Adult (YA) books are quite varied. Characters range from an assortment of standard high school characters—the outcast, the mean girls, the jocks, etc.—to deeply complicated kids. But whether a character is a jock, teen queen bee or complicated kid, you can individualize them so they don't sound like caricatures. Giving them individuality can make them standouts, not stock characters.

Character Voice

Young teens can still have young sounding, but not childlike voices. Older teens can sound more adult, but often embrace speech patterns associated with teens.

One of my favorites of those speech patterns is Teen Girl Speak which propels itself along at breakneck speed. Listen to those girls and you won't get half of what they say, but they 'like so totally' understand each other. (Or whatever the appropriate phrase is that teen girls are using when you read this.) Of course, not all teen girls fall into this pattern but it's a nice style to have in your arsenal.

I began directing *The Princess Diaries* audiobook series with Anne Hathaway. Bam! She just nailed that pattern…words spilling out one on top of the other, nearly shoving each other out of the way in order to be heard. It was great. But fast talk isn't the only key to that type of teen girl. Often there's the sense that every single thing they think or say is of the ABSOLUTE, UTMOST IMPORTANCE AND URGENCY!!! Add that psychological element to the voice, along with whatever other vocal elements and personality you give her, and you've got the start of a great teenage girl Character Voice.

Character Voice: Young Adult Workouts

The following is a fast-talking teen girl. While you may think you'll never have to read a character like this, you may be surprised. She might be the daughter of a hard-boiled detective in a tough crime novel, or she may be the daughter of a high society couple. So be prepared to read any character you might encounter and have fun with this one.

Text: OMIGOD!!

Omigod! I can't believe what happened. It's totally incredible!!! I never in a million, gazillion years thought anything like this would happen to me. I mean it's not that nice things don't happen to me. They do, but not so much. Okay, okay, I know good things happen, like when my dad got us tickets for a Broadway musical that I was dyyyyying to see. Oh, and my surprise birthday last year rocked, thank you again Maxine and Shani. So yeah, some good things happen.

Although teen boys can be presented as standard characters: the athletes, jocks, intellectuals, nerds, etc., each of them is still an individual.

In this teen guy selection, Justin and Sam, now approaching high school graduation, have been buddies for years. They are at the point of figuring out their divergent futures—one is excited, the other apprehensive. Give them Character Keys, their Character Voices, their objectives and actions.

Text: JUSTIN AND SAM

Justin casually sauntered over to his locker and dialed the combination. He was a senior now, and seniors didn't rush to class. They moved slow, too cool to worry about being a few minutes late for class. Especially if you were the quarterback of a winning varsity football team, which he was. The way he figured it they were lucky he showed up at all. As he was opening his locker, Sam walked over.

Sam was Justin's best friend. They'd met freshman year in science class. Sam changed Justin's view of what he used to call 'science geeks.' Although skinny and physically awkward when they met, Sam was a really cool guy, and without his help Justin would've never made it out of Biology class with anything higher than a D-. So, to kinda repay him, and also so they could hang together, Justin became his social rain maker, teaching him the social ropes of high school; getting him accepted where he never would have been on his own, especially with the girls. And that's how their relationship went, until senior year that is.

"Looks like somebody had a good time last night," Justin noted, looking over at his disheveled friend.

"Oh yeah!" Sam said emphatically, "Last night's party was excellent. Why didn't you come?"

"I had too much to do," Justin hedged.

"Well, you missed out," Sam said as he opened his locker. "It was pretty dope."

"Oh yeah," Justin laughed. "What, did you guys design some new robots or something?"

"Nope, no robots, my brother," Sam shot back, "but plenty of cute girls."

"Hmm," Justin said with a plastered-on smile, "looks like you science nerds are at the top of the social heap now."

"Yup," Sam replied, giving his friend a playful punch to the arm, oblivious to Justin's discomfort, "all you jocks will be working for us some day."

"Looks like it," Justin breathed.

"So," Sam asked, "did you decide yet about goin' to community college or taking that construction job?"

"Not sure yet," Justin replied, "If I went to college, I wouldn't even know what classes to take. But on the other hand, swinging a hammer for the rest of my life ain't that appealing either."

"Well, you know how I feel," Sam advised. "Carrying two-by-fours on your shoulder ain't no way to make a living."

"Yeah, I suppose. But we all can't get a scholarship to Stanford like you. But enough of this small talk," Justin said, changing the subject, "A bunch of us are getting together at Jim's house tomorrow night. His parents are away, and you are cordially invited. Lots of very hot young ladies attending."

"I wish I could make it but…"

"But what?" Justin asked.

Sam looked down at his shoes. "I…uh…promised Heidi, you know, from lab, that I'd, you know, help her with her science proj…"

"Oh," Justin cut in. "Then just forget it. It's not gonna be that big a deal."

"No, I'll go," Sam said, sensing Justin's disappointment, "I'll tell her to make it for another time."

"Nah," Justin said quickly, "you go do your thing. I know you've been macking on her for a while. Have a good time, bro."

Justin's mind swam in confusion as he looked in his locker door mirror and combed his hair. He wanted to feel good about Sam's new-found confidence with the girls, about his scholarship and bright future. And he did, but it was mixed with so much jealousy and resentment. Their high school days would be over soon, and the friend that he used to see as his underling would be in one of the best schools in the country, and from there go on to a successful and profitable career, while he'd be sawing plywood in the same town he was born in. The bitter feeling sucked, so, he did what any teenage male would do, pushed it down and ignored it.

"Who are you getting all prettied up for," Sam asked of his preening friend.

"Cindy Wyman," Justin sang, "the hottest girl in home room. Today's the day I make my move."

"I think you're over your head with that brainiac," Sam laughed. "The first time she starts talking about electrons and quarks, it's all over for you, my friend."

"Never underestimate animal charm, sonny. You just step back and watch the master at work."

"Okay, Sam cautioned, "but if you need any help, you know… with the electron stuff… I'm right here for you."[1]

Whether teens, kids, or adults, humans may be the predominate species you'll be voicing in an audiobook, but they may not be the only one.

---

[1] Text JUSTIN AND SAM by Neil Mitchell.

15

Character Voices for Animals

"Meow" means "woof" in cat.
—George Carlin

Animals can have a lot to say when they appear in books. And of course, if one is talking, it's got a personality.

Character Key

Identify gender, age, size, and outstanding personality traits. Is it old and wise? Is it a sly young trickster? Is it a jaded city slicker? Is it a helpful animal or a menacing one; a sneaky one, an eager one, or a gentle sweetheart? Is it the leader of a pack or a submissive being?

Character Voice

Use the animal's physicality and general nature to help create its voice.

First, identify the vocalization the animal makes, for example: the cat's low vibrational purr or higher pitched meow, the lion's guttural roar, the crow's sharp sounding caw.

Next, identify the pattern of the vocalization: the steadiness of the cat's purr, the extended roar of a lion that grows louder then lowers, the sharp repetitions of the crow's cawing, the rapid hoo-hoo sound of a chimp. Recordings of animal vocalizations are available on the web, so whatever the animal you need to voice, you can almost certainly hear its vocalization.

Use the size of the animal to decide the size and volume of its vocalization. The lion's roar will be big and loud, a petite starling could have a delicate little voice as might the tiny spider. Of course, if a book tells you the tiny little spider is domineering and has the voice of a giant or – as in one book I directed—it is a giant—make that spider big and bold.

You can use the animal's natural physical behaviors to determine the pacing of its speech. Does it lumber? Does it move swiftly? Does it pounce or leap? Think of the cat's slinking around, the lion's sudden leap, the bird's gliding on the air, the snake's slithering.

Give the animal its objective and action(s) and let it roar, hiss, growl, purr, meow, bark, hoot or chirp away.

Character Voice: Animals Workout

Read the paragraph below in the Character Voice of a mature 'confident' lion whose objective is a friendship, and give her an action.

Text: JUNGLE GUIDE

> I am here to offer my services as your jungle guide. I've been here for ages and know every single pathway. You won't make it alone you know. And I have longed for someone with whom I could have a decent conversation. By the way, I've eaten today, so no worries.

Read the same paragraph, with the same objective and action, but in the Character Voice of a snake, a crow, a cat or dog.

Of course in books, it's not only humans and animals that carry on conversations.

16

Character Voices for Fantasy Creatures, Chatty Objects, and Loquacious Nature

Earth laughs in flowers.
—Ralph Waldo Emerson

I n fantasy novels, everything speaks—elves, aliens, monsters, spoons, pots, pans, wind, brooks, trees, flowers—and of course, need I say it? If it's talking, it's got a personality and it wants something.

Character Key

Is the creature male, female, young, old, big or little? Does it come from another dimension? Is it funny? Arrogant? Shy? Highly intellectual? Slick? Snobby? Demure? Fussy? Bent on destruction? Eager to help?

Character Voice

For fantasy creatures: elves, monsters, trolls, etc. you can use all the vocal elements and speech patterns described earlier plus roars, squeaks, anything that reflects the creature's personality.

For Chatty Objects and Loquacious Nature, first identify an aspect of the character's natural sound. For example:

1. A metal pot can reverberate when struck.

   Hit the first syllable of a word the pot says hard and use a vibrato throughout the rest of word. Let the volume of your voice decrescendo, so it sounds like the reverb is fading.

2. A brook can make bubbly sounds.

   Keep your mouth very moist and do some baby-like vocalizations like plah plah plah or pluh pluh pluh. Keep your lips loose and let your tongue slap those sounds around in your mouth. It sounds 'bubbly,' like a babbling brook. You can use that sound on or between words or maybe just at the end of a sentence.

3. Wind is airy, whooshy. Use breathiness and whispers on the vowels to convey the wind's rush of air.

Next, use the character's size to determine the size of the vocalization.

1. A large pot gets a loud, extended reverberation, a small pot gets a little reverberation.

2. A large brook can have a big bubbling sound. A small one... little bubbling.

3. A very strong wind might have a big whooshing sound with a low vocalized undertone. A gentle breeze could have a delicate whispery whooshing.

Character Voices: Fantasy Creatures, Chatty Objects, and Loquacious Nature Workout

Read the following text in the Character Voice of the pot, the brook and the wind. Their objective is to keep everyone away. Their action is to warn.

Text: BEWARE

Beware. These beautiful bushes are not as they appear. They let their leaves sparkle in the sun, but they bear poisonous fruit. Stay away.

You can create a number of different characters by changing the position of your mouth.

Chose a Character Voice you've created for the pot, the brook or the wind. Read the BEWARE text again but this time as you speak, spread your lips wide and tight. Next, read it again but this time, purse your lips, pushing them way forward. Try different mouth positions. Each change creates a new sound, probably perfect for a group of weird creatures.

Take a bit of time and explore the various sounds you can make. Have fun. Play with different vocalizations. Explore your inner sound effects library. Mix and match sound elements, accents, cadences, personalities and mouth positions. A giant oak standing guard before a sacred forest can be a strong and unbendable force, with a rigid hard voice. Of course, if the book tells you that a giant oak has a small squeaky voice and it is embarrassed to speak because it was bullied in the past, you can forget the tough stuff.

More Character Voices: Fantasy Creatures, Chatty Objects, and Loquacious Nature Workouts

Read the following text as if it was being conveyed to an initiate. Pick a fantasy creature, chatty object, or a natural element of nature. Give it a Character Key, Character Voice, objective and action.

Text: THE WONDER

There is wonder in the woods.
Secrets revealed only to a few.
The brave or the foolish…
One never knows who is who,
And the path forward is always hidden from the seeker
and the sought.
It is forever, or for naught.
Your journey, no matter how anticipated,
No matter how unique or ill-fated is not predestined.
And it's outcome,
No matter its demands,
Though you didn't know,
Was always in your hands.

Let's create a threatening monster. Read the following with a husky sound and your mouth in a normal position, creating a mean and threatening monster. Make its objective to safeguard a sacred cave, and its action, to threaten.

Text: HORRIBLY UNWISE

To enter would be horribly unwise. No one is allowed to know the secret of the monsters.

Let's create another monster. This one is also threatening, but now as you speak, open your mouth extremely wide. The change of position changes your articulation as well as the sound. Read HORRIBLY UNWISE again using this new mouth position. Now you've got two monster voices. Perfect for two monster brothers!

Using the same initial husky sound, reposition your mouth so that your jaw and lips are extended forward, kind of like chimps move their lips. See what that does to your character.

Next try a grimace, or give it some clicks or slurps. Mix and match personalities using different mouth positions.

Congratulations! You're on your way to having your own monster clan, any of whom may be needed for a wild fantasy book.

You've got all the elements at the ready, now you just need to put them together.

PART SIX

PUTTING IT ALL TOGETHER

The art of making art, is putting it together.
—Stephen Sondheim

17

Longer Stories

Don't just go where you want to go,
but run, jump and dance as you are going.
                                        —Anonymous

You've acquired the techniques that enable you to create compelling, one-of-a-kind audiobook readings. Now it's time to apply those techniques, and your individual artistry, to longer stories that are closer to what you will be reading when you are contracted for a job.

Approach these stories as if you are doing a professional audiobook production.

- ◆ Record yourself so you can listen later. Use whatever recording equipment you have. A program like GarageBand will be fine.

- ◆ Use a good microphone and have a glass of room temperature water handy in case your mouth gets dry.

- ◆ Assess your performance and make note of what, if anything, you'd like to change and how you'll change it.

- ◆ Then record again and review. Do this until you're satisfied with the recording.

Give each story a tone and point of view. Give each character a Character Key, a Character Voice and Prompter Voice. Give them each an overall objective, scene objectives and actions. Respond to the imagery, the language style, and give it experiential immediacy. Note your choices on the manuscript. In short, use everything now at your command.

You may surprise yourself as some unexpected insights and unanticipated reactions emerge. They can connect you to the soul of the characters and the heart of the book in a way that can make you feel like you are flying.

The first story begins with a text you worked on earlier, HONDURAS. In this expanded version, the characters have dialogue. If you can use a Honduran accent for the Spanish dialogue, do so. And be sure you have the correct pronunciation for all words, names and foreign languages appearing in this and any story you work on.

Text: HONDURAS (Expanded)

We were surrounded by military police and escorted out of the airport to a waiting sedan. One of the policemen sat in front and we two were placed in the back. Sofia inquired in Spanish as to our destination but was met with silence bordering on disdain. That, combined with the lack of air-conditioning in the car, brought us to a higher level of concern and perspiration.

The car followed the pothole-scarred airport highway for about a half-hour before turning off at the older part of the capital city. The poverty, unseen by visitors flying in, was in full array all around us: toothless old ladies working the streets, younger ones like beasts of burden carrying all manner of things: bundles of old clothes wrapped in twine, buckets of unspeakable liquids. Sewage and garbage were strewn everywhere. We quickly turned a corner and were presented with a most ominous sight, a combination police station and what I assumed to be a jailhouse but was in fact one of the huge federal prisons, a monolithic yellowing ugly concrete structure forty feet high and topped by watch towers at the corners and razor wire in between. The situation was getting increasingly dire by the moment.

The car circled to the entrance of the prison, an enormous medieval-looking iron gate manned by two sentries in combat uniforms. The driver stopped, leaned out the window and mumbled something to one of them in colloquial Spanish that I didn't understand. The gate, with a loud clanking noise, began to rise slowly. We were directed to a parking area. The car stopped. The officer in front opened the door for us and we emerged sweaty and concerned and were led to a stone archway, the door to the building. Dim hallway lights reflected off of the granite bricks of the ancient construction, foreboding and evil.

A couple of turns and we came to the office of the *Comandante*, the boss. We entered and were ushered into the big man's inner sanctum, an institutional-looking gray room with a gray chair, gray file cabinets and a very gray *Comandante* who was seated at a steel desk, also gray. General Perez couldn't have been more than 5ft. 1in., a dead ringer for Danny DeVito, with very greasy hair. On the desk, in full view, was my .45.

The Comandante sat us down and, in rapid Spanish, got right to the point: "*Ustedes han entrado en la soberanía de Honduras con un arma ilegal!*" he bellowed. "You have entered the sovereignty of Honduras with an illegal weapon." The halls echoed with his screaming. A moment passed, deathly quiet. Although I knew Spanish pretty well, Sofia did most of the talking to other Spanish speakers, unless I had to. Now, she stared at this small man. She was scared to death, but very deliberately and patiently spoke up, in Spanish.

"*Por favor Comandante*," she began, her voice betraying only the slightest tremor, "we gave the gun to the pilot. We didn't try to smuggle it into the country! And," she paused, sitting up ramrod straight, "as a citizen of Honduras I am embarrassed by this action towards a foreigner." The ensuing hush was palpable. "*Señorita*," the *Comandante* began with a smile. "I see that you are a true *patriota*. However, the law forbids the importation of handguns into our country no matter the method. And the law is the law and you and El Señor broke it." The military man rose up to his full height and solemnly declared: "I have no choice but to confiscate the weapon." I cringed. I gripped the arms of the chair I was in, forcing myself to stay seated. I turned to Sofia and, thru her, tried to appeal to the man's sense of family. "Tell him, Sofia, that the gun belonged to my dad who gave it to me before he died."

No go. It was apparent from the way he was fondling it that he had taken a shine to the weapon and wanted to keep it for himself. I wanted to pick it up off the desk and...

He smiled, perhaps knowing what I was thinking and almost daring me to try. Sofia put her hand on my leg and whispered, "For now, let us leave quietly while we can and not antagonize the man." Good advice. And that's what we did.

We took a taxi back to the airport, picked up our things, rented a car and began the arduous drive along the narrow, pot-holed mountain roads to Sofia's parents' place in San Pedro Sula. I was fuming and needed to concentrate and bear down so as not to exceed the speed limit and knock a *carreta* off the road. "That son of a bitch wants the gun for himself. The law is bullshit."

"Danny, please, let's talk to my brother Ricardo when we get to my home," Sofia said, trying to calm me down. "He may know someone who could help us." I spent the trip fantasizing about squashing the general under my foot, totally oblivious to the mountain beauty around us.

We settled in at Sofia's parents' house on the outskirts of the city, but I couldn't get the gun off my mind. It was mine; it had been in my possession a long time. It had been serviced and made very accurate by a U.S. army gunsmith and no undersized *Comandante* was going to steal it from me!

Ricardo, Sofia's brother, was a big shot with the Autoridad Portuaria, the area's port authority. Sofia's dad had called him after hearing about the incident. He came right over. He suggested we contact a friend of his, a local attorney by the name of Señor Delgado who might intercede on our behalf. We did and met with Sr. Delgado in the heat of the day at a small *taverna* in town. San Pedro Sula back then was a quaint, bustling village caught in the humidity of the tropics and totally without air-conditioning. *Tavernas* offered a respite from the brutal heat, being dark and featuring numerous ceiling fans that created a cooling breeze. We sat near the doorway and waited for the arrival of the attorney. An interesting bouquet of cinnamon and sweat filled the room.

Sr. Delgado glided in wearing the standard attorney's uniform of a white linen suit, straw fedora and manicured mustache—he could have stepped out of an old Peter Lorre movie. Ricardo had assured us this fellow knew his way around the military and could help us.

"*Hola*, Sr. Delgado!" Ricardo rose from his chair and greeted the man. The attorney approached us, and they shook hands. "You look well, Ricardo. Government work must be agreeing with you." Ricardo smiled and introduced us. Sr. Delgado warmly took my hand. We sat down and ordered the local beer, a Pilsner style, very flavorful but most importantly, very cold. Ricardo went on to explain the problem. When he finished, I looked at this kindly gentleman. "Sr. Delgado, *¿me puede ayudar?*" "Can you help me?"

It turned out that Sr. Delgado knew the Comandante personally and was able to assure us of a successful outcome. "No *te preocupes!*" "Don't worry." He raised his glass in a toast and we did likewise. "*Salud!*" That was encouraging.

He then quoted his fee, 2500 *lempiras*, which sounded like a lot until realized it was actually only about $75. The plan was for Sr. Delgado to speak privately with Perez and then Sofia and I would join in.

And so it was. The next day, feeling pretty confident, we drove back to the police station. I was prepared to bribe the General if I had to, to get my gun back. The lawyer was there already and in with him. We anxiously waited outside his office. The lethargic ceiling fan did nothing to cool off my anger and frustration. Then, abruptly, the door to Perez' office opened. Now Sr. Delgado was not a particularly tall man but when the two of them walked out, arms wrapped around each other like two ill-fitting lovers, I could see the lawyer's smiling face way, way above the General's greasy dome. I didn't know if this was a good sign or a bad one. I soon found out.

The two men disengaged themselves from each other. The *Comandante* gestured for us to follow him back into his office. Sr. Delgado, with the universal flourish that indicates "this way," and with a whispered "*Siga, siga!*"—"Follow him!" —made sure we understood the intent of the military man's order and moved us along.

We entered the now-familiar office and sat down. Perez sat down too and looked at us for a long time before speaking.

Something didn't feel right.

Now the general assumed, wrongly so, that I did not speak or understand Spanish; Sofia would translate most everything that was spoken to be certain I grasped it.

"Your attorney is a man of reason and sensibilities," he began pleasantly. Too pleasantly I thought. My antennae were now fully extended, my confidence having slowly slipped away. "Together we have arrived at a way to dispense with all this unpleasantness. Now that the two of you realize that the gun you brought into our country is illegal and subject to confiscation, we will not prosecute you for this crime." He smiled benignly, like a father forgiving his son for banging up the family car. He seemed genuinely disappointed at our lack of a show of gratitude but continued. "And we will return to you the ammunition that accompanied the gun, being that the possession of cartridges does not constitute a crime." And with that, he opened a desk drawer and pulled out two green boxes, old and heavily soiled, and definitely not mine.

By now, I was pissed! I totally erupted! I left my chair as if attached to a rocket, and blurted out, "*Eso no es me marca!!*" "THOSE CARTRIDGES ARE NOT MINE!!" The *Comandante*, turning a dreadful red color, rose to his full five foot one height, glared up at me. "You are," he spit out, "both deceitful and despicable, and for pretending not to understand the Mother tongue, you are to be placed under house arrest and fined an enormous sum of money!" With that, he motioned to his two Sergeants-at-Arms posted at the doorway. Sofia screamed!

The lawyer rose from his chair as if to intercede but by then the two guards were all over me as I tried to evade them. The lawyer hollered at Sofie: "*Calmase!!* Tell him not to fight with them; they will shoot him for resisting arrest!" I realized this was probably true and stopped long enough to allow myself to be handcuffed. I whispered to Sofia, "Call the American Consulate," puckered a kiss goodbye, and was led off. Maybe not the wisest thing, but as I was being pushed through the office door, I couldn't resist turning and mouthing "F--k you" to the two of them.[1]

The following story is one you haven't worked on so you can approach it with completely fresh eyes and responses.

Text: MY POET

Adrienne stared out the living room window. It was one of those beautiful, unexpected but hoped for, New York nights. Snow was falling heavily, integrating itself into the fabric of the city. Fresh and white, it was glistening under the signs and lights that advertised everything from the most elegant restaurants to the bodegas that served the busy citizens of Manhattan. Need a sandwich? A soda? A bottle of bleach? The corner bodega is your go-to spot. It was something she missed whenever she left the city, but especially when she visited L.A. How could people get along without a *bodega* on every corner? She was actually excited when she spotted one while on the way to a little, hidden-away theater. She made a quick stop and bought an overpriced bottle of water, a pack of tissues and something she couldn't remember. Unimportant things. Things she didn't need but that allowed her to mentally pay homage to the bodegas of New York. The water would come in handy in the tiny, overheated theater she was attending that night. The show was not memorable, even though her boyfriend did have a small role in it.

Her apartment on the West Side was a decent size, a lucky find in New York. The compact living room featured her main indulgence, a mahogany bookshelf filled with books. Her great grandmother had collected the *Books of Wonder*, a poor person's version of the *Encyclopedia Britannica*. The books had

---

[1] Text HONDURAS by Ira Marks.

become family treasures; treasures her mom had inherited from her own mother. Adrienne had a vivid memory of doing a report for class on South America. She'd opened a *Book of Wonder* and landed on a section about Paraguay and Uruguay. At eleven-years-old, Adrienne found the names evocative and powerful. The soft-toned black and white images of rural landscapes seemed mysterious, and the foreign words— *pampas* and *gauchos*—thrilled her. It was then she'd begun to understand the power of books and decided that in the future she would have her own library. Her books and her piano were the only possessions she really cared about. The piano, like the books, was not an indulgence. It was a necessity.

She was looking at a spot on the window when Michael called. She'd noticed that a bit of snow had blended with a smudge on the window's outer layer of grime, creating interesting patterns. One looked like a weirdly evolved bacteria with long feelers searching for a place to rest, another like a floating lily detached from its pad.

"Hey," Michael said, when Adrienne picked up the phone. "What's happening?"

"Nothing special," she said, still staring at the smudge.

"This is some snowstorm."

"I know. Beautiful right?"

"It is," Michael said, "even though I miss the constant sunshine of L.A."

"Oh come on. You were only there for a two-week run. You would have gotten tired of all that sunlight."

Adrienne had met Michael a little over a year ago. She'd been trying to hail a cab for twenty minutes during morning rush hour when he suddenly appeared on the opposite side of the street and, as if by magic, a cab pulled right up to him.

She had the green, raced across the street and yanked the cab door open. "Which way are you going?" she demanded of the passenger.

"Uh... 50th and 5th?" he said as if it was a question.

"Perfect. I've been waiting twenty minutes! This should have been my cab, but he just pulled up to you, so can you please drop me at 47th and Madison, or I'll probably lose the biggest chance of my life and wind up homeless...out on the street with nowhere to go and also I...."

"This I've gotta hear," he said laughing. "Hop in."

"Really? That worked?" she said, noticing how cute the guy was, and starting to laugh herself.

"The light's changin' lady," the cabbie growled. "You wanna get us killed? He said get in, so get in."

She hurried in and by the time they reached her office, she knew he was an actor and that he had one sister. He knew she had a job in advertising, but her passion was writing, and she too had one sister.

They'd exchanged numbers and been pretty near insepa-rable for a year since that day, except for living in different apartments.

Michael was a working actor. Good looking and talented, twenty-six years old to her twenty-four. Not a star—"yet" he'd remind her—but between commercials, theater and voice-over jobs, he kept busy.

"What are you up to?" she asked, turning away from the window.

"Page five of the new show I'm auditioning for."

"Good part?"

"I'm hoping I show up on page six," he laughed. "Actually, it is a good part, and the audition is tomorrow."

"Otherwise you'd be coming over, right?"

"You know it." he said, making his voice low and sexy.

She loved that voice. It was the voice actors and singers could use to make women go nuts.

"Don't do that." she said.

"What?"

"You know. THE VOICE!! It's snowing, it's cold, and neither of us is leaving our nice warm apartment. So pleeease... don't do it."

"Okay, okay," he said in a still sexy voice but laughing. "I've got to get back to the script. But first, what about you? Any new writing from my poet?"

"Ummmm," she said. "I've been busy looking at snow make love to grime on my window."

Michael was supportive of her and her writing. He was like her dad in that way. Her dad was her rock. He'd backed her getting her own apartment when her mother had freaked out at the idea. And though she'd majored in psychology and her mother thought she was nuts, her father was supportive of her desire to go into show business.

She'd signed with an agent shortly after graduating from college. He'd booked her first gig in a small club out of town, the Lion Club.

"You're good," the agent had said. "It's a cool spot, and the crowd will have a great time."

She didn't have any musical arrangements but that didn't matter because the club didn't have any musicians. It would be just her at the piano, singing her original songs. She was excited, but nervous. Her songs were pop styled but sometimes obtuse and issue oriented, not necessarily the stuff for what turned out to be a heavy drinking crowd—not that crowd was the word she would have chosen to describe the small group seated at tables and at the bar.

She took the stage for her first set, and the boozers gave her their full attention for all of two seconds, then they turned to each other, drank, laughed, smooched and – just as her agent had predicted – they had a great time! Mortified, she bravely went on, not that anyone noticed. She left the stage when her set was over, to an accompanying four teeny-tiny claps. The bartender shook his head and looked at her with sympathy. She couldn't tell if it was sympathy for her or for the crowd.

In her hotel room above the club, she called her dad.

"How'd it go?" he asked eagerly.

"I bombed," she said, trying to joke. "But what's worse is that I have to do another set in an hour."

"Was it that bad?"

"Worse."

"What did you play?"

"My best songs."

"Oh! Your deep stuff," her dad said, making her laugh. "Wrong set for that crowd. They're drinkers, not thinkers." Just revise your next set. Don't focus on the failure."

"I'm not. Well, maybe a little."

"Look, you're great. Go revise the set. They're drinking right? They're out for a good time. They don't want to hear about the world's problems. They want to hear some up-tempo-let's-have-fun-stuff. You do know some of those right?"

"I do," she said a little morosely. "They're not mine, but I know them."

"So you flopped," he said, making her laugh at the word. "Go back for your next set and show them how good you are."

She returned to the Lion Club, now her personal Roman Coliseum. Armed with a new set, she strode up to the stage, sat down and rocked out. After the first few bars of music, a couple of people turned their heads to watch her. Then others did, and soon she had everybody's attention. She kept the set up-tempo and fun and left the stage to everyone cheering and the bartender giving her a big thumbs up.

Her success was both a blessing and a curse. A blessing in that it fortified her commitment to pursue a career in music. The curse was the same. She got a few more gigs but performing that way did not make her happy. She wanted to say something more with her music. Not that it mattered, because soon after, her agent quit the business, and her few club dates dried up. Needing to pay the rent, she applied for a job as an assistant in an ad agency. She knew she had a way with words, and she had her psychology degree. She figured at least she'd be working in a job that dealt with language and human behavior. After a year she began writing copy. One of the other copy writers, Tommy, was also the jingle guy, so as much as she loved music, she didn't put herself forward as a jingle writer. First of all, she didn't want to upset Tommy any further being that he was already resentful of her promotion to copy writer. Second, she never saw her lyric style as jingle material, and third, no one had ever asked her.

"I seem to have talent for describing the greatness of kitchenware," she'd told Michael recently. "You know, pots and pans that transform whatever you cook into culinary masterpieces, or your money back. Guaranteed!"

"Funny," he teased, "because you don't own any pots and pans. Your kitchen cabinets are full of files."

"Yeah but I can make you want that pot even though you have five others."

"Endearing."

"It's a job. And it pays for the splendor of my apartment."

She didn't exactly dislike her job, but she definitely didn't love it. The agency owner, Richard Washington, was a good guy. But her success at the agency was like when she'd killed it at the Lion Club. It wasn't 'her.' And the rewards—the applause at the club or the paycheck at the job—were not enough to crush her desire for more. Still, she tried reminding herself that she was one of the lucky ones.

"I get it," she'd told her sister once when they were downing coffee at the corner coffee shop. "Tons of people would kill to be in my situation."

"Yes. So why can't you just be happy about it?" Her sister was perennially happy.

"Because I can't. I don't know why. I see the issues we're all dealing with, and I just have to write about them. I didn't choose to be like this, I just am. I'm not even saying I'm good at writing those songs. But…"

"But they have meaning for you. I get it," her sister laughed. "You were always a little weird. And you won't even show me the songs you're writing. Me!!! Your own sister."

"I will," she said. "I promise."

The evening after the snowstorm, Adrienne and Michael were out to dinner at their favorite Chinese food restaurant on the East Side when Michael asked when she was going to try to get her music out there again.

"I hardly have time to work on it now."

"Really? That doesn't sound like you."

"Me? Ha. I'm the girl who's now writing about a new product to clean your drains."

"Seriously, are you still writing your own stuff?"

"I am," she laughed, "still writing 'stuff,' as you call it."

"Sorry. Your poetic gems."

"That's better," she said.

"How's work?" he asked.

"Sometimes…I just wish…I could figure out how to make the two me's work as one person. I feel split. I'm the "fix your drains" girl and…."

"My poet," he said, taking her hand. "You'll do it. Stay positive. Make room for the unexpected. They say God works in mysterious ways."

"When did you get religious?" she laughed.

"About three hours ago," he smiled, "when I landed the lead in a new show at Lincoln Center. This is our celebratory dinner."

"Oh Michael. That's incredible. I'm so happy for you." She leaned over and kissed him. "Mmmm. You taste of Mu Shu Beef. Yummy."

They went back to her apartment. Later, after Michael had fallen asleep, she felt restless. She couldn't stop thinking of what he'd said, "make room for the unexpected." She poured a glass of wine, sat down at her computer and wrote:

Does the center just keep spinning?

Are we always on the turn?

Ever seeking liberation, and avoidance of the burn?

Or are we all just dancers on a tiny pirouette?

Round and round and wondering, is this really all we get?

Are the spirits that entice us merely phantoms that compel?

Are they access routes to heaven, are they messengers from hell?

If everything's conception, if we play it as we feel,

If reality's perception, what we see's the only deal.

Michael was still asleep when she woke up the next morning. She showered, dressed, kissed his sleeping face goodbye and grabbed a cab. The streets were slushy now, and the white snow had turned an unlovely gray. The agency Adrienne worked for was on the twentieth floor of a sleek building, a glass and steel edifice that looked out over Madison Avenue. Happily, the coffee, bagels and Danish cart was in front of the building. She grabbed a cup of coffee and headed in.

Her office was small but she liked it, mostly because it had a window from which she could look out and see the endless flow of traffic heading uptown and the flow of people—all moving in a great stream of energy and purpose, everyone unique and yet part of something greater. Today though, everyone was less flowing and streaming and more tromping through the slush.

Adrienne had a meeting scheduled for 10 a.m. in her office with the art director, Brian, to go over the copy and artwork for a new drain cleaner commercial. When Brian didn't show she buzzed his phone, but no one picked up, so she walked over to Debbie's office. The office manager was in her mid-forties and though she'd been in New York for at least ten years, she'd retained much of her Southern accent, which Adrienne found totally endearing.

"Mornin' honey," Debbie drawled as Adrienne came in.

"Back at you," Adrienne responded. "Have you seen Brian? We were supposed to have a meeting."

Debbie checked her schedule. "He and Tommy are in a meetin' with Richard now. Oh, wait…you're s'posed to be there too honey."

"Really? No one told me."

"I'm sorry. Tommy said he'd let you know."

"Well, he didn't. What's the meeting about?"

"A PSA for climate change. You know, risin' sea levels and all that."

"Climate change?" Adrienne asked, suddenly on alert.

"That's what they told me," Debbie answered.

"Where are they?"

"Music room..."

"Thanks," Adrianne said, and hurried towards the music room.

"You're welcome," Debbie called out.

The door to the music room was closed, so Adrienne opened it and walked in.

"Adrienne," said Richard in his basso voice. "You're late."

"I'm sorry. I wasn't told about the meeting."

"Really?" said Tommy, his voice a little too loud and a little too surprised sounding. "I messaged you."

"Oh?" she said quickly. "I never got it. Can you fill me in? Debbie said it's for a PSA."

"It's about climate change," Tommy said. "And if it catches on, there's a chance it could be used at an upcoming climate change event that..."

"They want," Richard interrupted, "something that doesn't sound commercial. Something with a retro sixties feel in terms of style, passion and ideas. Capture the old folks and the new generation of activists."

"We want to get the music right," Brian said, "before we start putting together the visuals."

"What do you have so far?" Adrienne asked.

"A few ideas, but nothing's clicking," Richard said. "Show her what we've got Tommy."

Tommy sat down at the piano and began playing.

"We can bring the world back on a better course,
There's no time to wait around..."

"I see," Adrienne said.

"It's just the beginning idea," Tommy said defensively.

"I understand," she said, sitting next to him on the piano bench in a way that made him move to the side. "What about these chords and this feel?" She began to play something that sounded closer to a sixties' sensibility.

"Interesting," Richard said leaning in. "Where would you take that?"

"Well," she said, still playing. "I've been working on something at home." She expected to feel exposed, uncomfortable. But instead she found a renewed sense of bravery. What the heck, she thought. What's the worst they could do to me, and began to sing:

Momma Earth and Poppa Sky,
Gettin' it together, givin' us one more try.
Here we are, at the edge of time
As the dancers slowly move in place
Vision signals, silence is the crime
As destiny cries out to the human race.
We're calling…
Momma Earth and Poppa Sky,
Gettin' it together, givin' us one more try.
Momma Earth and Poppa Sky.
Momma Earth and Poppa Sky.

When she finished, the room was quiet until Richard broke the silence.

"You wrote this?" he asked. "This is your work?"

"Yes," she said, unsure of what he'd say next.

He started to laugh. "And I had no idea! Play it again."

"Damn!" he said when she finished. "Where have you been hiding?"

"I write these at home. For me. When you said the sixties feel, I thought maybe this one would work."

"It does for me," Richard said.

"Me too," Brian agreed. "Can you program a few other instruments?"

"Not very well."

Richard turned to Tommy. "Okay then. You lay down drum and guitar tracks. She'll play and sing and we'll shoot a demo over to the client."

"No problem," Tommy mumbled.

Richard and Brian stood up, and as they left the room, Brian smiled at Adrienne. "Nice work," he said. "Really nice work."

It wasn't until 6 p.m., after she'd arrived home and was told they'd landed the job, that Adrienne called Michael. "I'm not just your poet anymore," she said, then told him everything. "It was the sixties groove that did it. I'm modern retro."

"So I have to share you with the world now?"

"You've gotta welcome the unexpected! Right?"

"Until I die," he said softly in THE VOICE, "you'll always be *my* poet."

"Come over," she whispered.

"I'm already on my way."[1]

You've acquired the skills that enable you to personally connect with any story. You can give an audiobook its tone and a book narrator a point of view. You are able to create experiential immediacy and bring characters and scenes to life. You're adept at developing distinguishable Character Voices and giving those characters objectives and actions. You're skilled at using imagery appropriately to fire your listeners' imaginations, and you can convince them that a stone can speak with emotion, maybe even with an accent. You can make nonfiction rich and interesting, and you are confident about your work.

Now all you've got to do is be heard.

---

[1] Text MY POET by Taro Meyer and Neil Mitchell.

PART SEVEN

GETTING DOWN TO BUSINESS

Beautiful things make money.

—Geoffry Beene

18

Your Career

Success is when preparation and opportunity meet.
—Bobby Unser

Getting Heard

Everything you do to develop your art is simultaneously a business move. The more you explore your creativity, the more you stimulate your imagination, and the more you hone your technique, the better your work will be. And the better the work, the greater the professional opportunities you'll be able to handle.

Publishers and producers are always interested in finding new talent, but they'll want to hear what you can do before hiring you. You may be skilled at short-form commercials, animation or documentary narration but that doesn't automatically translate to the skills needed for long form audiobook work.

Unless you're a well-known performer or audiobook actor, you'll need to create a demo—a recording that specifically showcases your talent for audiobook narration. You don't need to add sound effects or music. Just make your reading compelling by using all the techniques you've acquired. You want whomever you're introducing yourself to, to know that you can handle an audiobook professionally and creatively. You need a demo and you want it to shine.

Your Demo should showcase your ability to:

1. Establish a Tone and Point of View.

2. Create Experiential Immediacy.

3. Develop believable characters, with identifiable Character Voices.

4. Create dialogue interaction.

5. Read nonfiction in an interesting manner.

Your Demo should include:

1. Three to five selections that are at least two minutes long.[1]

2. Different genres to demonstrate that you can handle a wide range of audiobooks, e.g., novels, biographies, children's books, young adult, history, adventure, instructional, fantasy, etc.

3. At least one selection in first person and one in third person.

4. Selections that have both narrative and dialogue, at least one with dialogue between a man and a woman.

5. A selection that shows you can handle humor – if you can. Not jokes, but light, humorous material.

6. Children's, Young Adult or Fantasy, if you can do kids' voices, monsters, etc.

7. The names and authors of any copyrighted material you are using, with copyright information at the end of the demo.

Give each selection a definitive ending so the listener has a sense of completion and knows that you can create a story arc, taking it from the beginning to the end.

If you're contacting someone, perhaps via e-mail, to submit your work, provide a link to your demo and resume (if you're not uploading

---

[1] Under the Fair Use doctrine, it is generally understood that one can use a small portion of material from a published work for demo and non-commercial purposes. However, since 'small portion' is subjective, any time you use copyrighted material, be sure you seek advice of copyright counsel.

to a platform with an established format) so they can easily access your work.

Your demo should start strong and stay strong! You want producers' ears to perk up as soon as they hear you read. Think of pop songs. They catch you right away or they usually don't make it.

When I was reviewing demo submissions for an important multi-book project, *The Inheritance Cycle* by Christopher Paolini, most of the demos that had been submitted to me had typical and, frankly, uninteresting reads. There was nothing unique or captivating in the performances. After hearing one or two selections, I would move on to the next demo.

Then I listened to a demo by an actor named Gerard Doyle. I was immediately drawn in. I could hear the point of view in each selection. His Character Voices were interesting and diverse. He created experiential immediacy by giving moment-to-moment readings that made the stories vibrant and made me want to keep listening. I was riveted. After I heard the entire demo, I called the Executive Producer and told him we'd found our actor. He knew Gerard's work and agreed that he would be terrific. And he was. *The Inheritance Cycle* audiobooks garnered great industry recognition including an Audie Award nomination, the American Library Notable Children's Recordings List, an Earphones Award, the YALSA Teen Top Ten List, and the Amazing Audiobook for Young Adults List. And it was because he made his demo shine that he landed the project.

Pre-Recording

Today's technology allows you to record at home. If you can't do that yet, or prefer not to handle the tech, there are professional studios where you can record your demo with an experienced engineer. Make sure the studio has a soundproof recording booth and that you have a good idea of how much time you'll need to complete your recording. Get a written statement of the studio's fees prior to reserving time.

There are other options allowing you to work with an engineer from your own studio. You can arrange a zoom session in which the engineer, at a different location, can access your computer remotely and run your recording program. Also, there are internet remote recording options, such as Source-Connect, enabling an engineer in a different location to record you at their end. As with a recording studio, if you choose one of these options, be sure to confirm the fees.

If you record at home in your own studio, do so in a quiet area—no buses and cars zooming by, no dogs barking, or kids racing through the house. Many people use a spare closet to set up a small, low-cost professionally acceptable recording studio. There are numerous books and online tutorials that can guide you to setting up your studio with reasonably priced baffling (room noise reduction insulation), good microphones, recording programs, etc. There are also instructions for recording and editing, but technology is always changing; specs and the most appropriate programs and equipment may change with it. Always check for the latest information.

In order to get ready for your recording session, here's a checklist:

1. Headphones: Some actors like recording with headphones, others don't. Try it both ways and see what works for you.

2. Prepare the manuscript with a font large enough to read comfortably.

3. Research the proper pronunciation of unfamiliar words, proper names, and foreign words or phrases.

4. Be sure that the selections have no textual errors. This is very important when you're recording professionally. Even when books are extremely well written and edited, errors can occur. Sometimes you can query a publisher, but it may take a while to get an answer. If you think the possible error(s) might present a problem, choose a different selection.

5. Rehearse before your recording session. Notate the text with any notes you want to remember. Color code the Character Voices if it helps you quickly identify who will be speaking next.

6. Set up your tablet, computer, or the manuscript if you're reading from a printed book, so you can maintain your same head position relative to the microphone.

The Recording

1. Create an opening at the beginning of your demo on a separate track. (A track is a single stream of sound.)

2. State your name and contact information.

3. For each selection state the name of the book and author.

4. Record each selection on a separate track. That way it will be easier to reorganize the readings if you want to.

The Recording Session (useful information for both demo and professional recording)

It can be surprising that recording is very physically demanding. You have to sit still for long periods of time, stay in the same position and move around as little as possible. That takes a lot of energy. So be prepared for it.

1. Wear soft, comfortable clothing, nothing starched or stiff. You want to be as comfortable as possible. Also, stiff clothing can make little noises with the slightest of movements. You may not notice them, but your microphone will.

2. Have something to eat about an hour prior to your session. That can help reduce stomach noises. Those noises are very surprising to new audiobook actors. Unless there's some real seismic activity going on in our stomachs, we don't normally hear those noises, but they are gurgling away much of the time. The microphone amplifies those little gurgles, so on playback it can be a bit of a shocker; you can hear real rumbling. Stomach noises are called borborygmi. Those borborygmi are worse when the stomach or digestive tract is empty. Surprisingly, I've found that a few bites of a bagel can calm actors' stomach noises. If they don't stop, try

putting a pillow or soft cushion over your stomach. That may muffle the sounds.

3. Forgo dairy products, they create phlegm.

4. Don't eat sticky food like nut butters.

5. Keep water on hand. Drink it at room temperature—not iced.

6. If you get mouthy—you're making little mouth noises as you read—a few sips of water or a bite of a green apple can help, so have that on hand.

7. Turn off your phone(s) and if possible, don't have one in the studio. It might ring or vibrate just when you are recording your best take. (A take is a single performance of a particular amount of the script.)

8. Do a sound check prior to recording the demo to make sure that you are in the best position vis-à-vis your microphone and that you're getting the best sound.

9. Sit in a comfortable chair that doesn't move or squeak. Everyone moves slightly as they read, so if your chair squeaks you'll have squeaks in the production. If the squeaks are between words, you can edit them out, but it's harder when they're under words.

10. It's important to maintain the same position of your head relative to the microphone throughout the session. A small shift may not be noticeable, but if you change position too much, if you move closer to or further from the microphone, if you turn your head to the side or up or down, your sound will likely change.

11. Mark the position of your chair on the floor. That way when you take a break, if you move your chair to get up, or your session is continuing the next day, you can put the chair back in the same position it was originally in. This will keep the chair's position relative to the mic the same, and thus help keep your sound the same.

12. Keep your voice at a consistent decibel level. You can have emotional and range dynamics, but you don't want the recording level—the volume at which you are being recorded—to suddenly jump up too loudly in one spot then become very soft in another. And you don't want to overload the microphone, which will give your great take a suddenly awful, unusable sound.

13. Do as many takes as you need to get your best reading. If you are not sure that you like a particular take, record the material again. You can listen later and select the best version.

14. Number the takes. You can note the take number on your manuscript at the spot you begin a take so you can locate each take. You may want to use different portions of several takes to create your final reading. If you're not skilled at editing, you can find books or online courses that will guide you, or consider contacting a professional editor.

15. Record a few seconds of room tone (RT) while you are outside of the booth or recording space. Room tone is the recorded sound of the recording space you are using when you are not speaking. It is used when you need to create a little more room between words on the recording, to adjust pacing, or to fill in where a noise has been edited out. Some actors have recorded room tone while sitting in the booth and not speaking. When done that way, however, the microphone will likely pick up small breathing noises, stomach noises, tiny chair squeaks, etc., which will make it hard to find a clean spot to use if needed.

16. Take breaks. If you are getting tired, if you need a bit of air, or to stretch, take a break. Get up and move around.

17. Listen to your demo to ensure you are happy with it and re-record any sections you want to redo prior to editing.

Editing Your Demo

Since many publishing and production companies require actors to handle the whole production, it's best to provide a clean and well edited demo, demonstrating your ability to deliver a finished product.

1. You can tighten or open sections that need some tweaking. You want the edit to reflect your reading—your pacing, your pauses, etc.

2. Be sure the reading is clean: no slurps, nose snorts, borborygmi, shirt crinkles or chair squeaks. There are apps and plug-ins that can help remove extraneous noises.

3. Be sure the recording level is consistent. The sound should stay at the same level throughout, no sudden jumps, no overloading the microphone. Your reading can and should have dynamics—the changes in vocal volume that are responsive to the emotional shifts in your reading—but nothing that suddenly changes the level excessively. You can find many online tutorials about the technical aspects of recording.

4. If you find any problems, fix them or re-record the troublesome spots and edit them in.

5. If you are not adept at the technical end of things—recording, editing, mastering—whether for your demo or future professional bookings, you can contract that work out.

Your Resumé

Styles change, so make sure your resumé is formatted according to the latest style. If you've recorded audiobooks, whether for commercial purposes or as a volunteer, list the titles, authors, and publishers' name and provide links to the works. If you've received positive reviews, provide links to them and include some of their best lines, naming the sources. Include your Theater, Film, TV, Recording, Voice Over (VO) and Commercials credits. Note any special skills: accents, languages, knowledge of scientific or medical terminology, etc. If you're slim on professional experience, or have none and are new to the business, include your college experience and/or local theater productions if you have those. The fact that you haven't done audiobooks previously won't matter if your demo shows that you can do them now.

Non-Paying and Volunteer Work

If you haven't done any professional audiobook work, do some for free. Not only will it pump up your resumé, but it will give you valuable practice. And some of the free work serves such wonderful causes that you'll feel great about doing it. Following are three interesting volunteer opportunities:

Learning Ally (learningally.org), formerly: Recording for the Blind and Dyslexic, RFB&D, is an excellent place to start. The company serves "…more than 300,000 K-12, college and graduate students, veterans and lifelong learners—all of whom cannot read standard print due to blindness, visual impairment, dyslexia, or other learning disabilities." They use volunteers in numerous states across the country, and if you're so inclined, you can also help with preparing the books and assisting in the production.

Libri Vox (librivox.org), which records books in the public domain, uses volunteers from all over the world.

Children's Library Readings. Volunteer to read to children at your local library. Libraries often have storytelling times and will generally be pleased to have you participate. If your local library doesn't have a storytime for children, perhaps you can launch one. Reading aloud, especially to kids, provides great feedback on what is working in your reading and what's not.

Representation

If you have an agent: Let your agent know you want to be submitted for audiobooks. Many agencies have voiceover departments under which the audiobook category falls. Some agencies don't work in the audiobook field. If that's the case, ask if your agency is comfortable with another agency handling that part of your career. If so, reach out to agents that do handle audiobooks.

If you don't have an agent: Thanks to the internet, there are professional opportunities you can access on your own, without the benefit of an agent.

Getting Work

Publishers, Producers, Production Houses

You want to get your demo heard by the publishing executives, producers, and production houses who oversee or contribute to casting decisions.

Check the website of the company or producer you are hoping to submit your demo to. They may have specs and requirements that you'll need to follow.

Online Casting

There are numerous online casting sites to which you can upload your demo, samples of work done and your resumé. They connect audiobook actors (also referred to as Narrators) with prospective producers and/or authors.

For some of these companies, as previously noted, you'll be expected to serve as the producer of the audiobook, providing an edited, mastered, finished project. If you prefer not to handle the post-production or it is financially advantageous for you to record more books and contract out the post-production, you can team up with a good editor. Since you can send them the files of your finished read, you don't have to be in the same location. If you don't know any editors, you can find them on online freelance sites such as upwork.com or fiverr.com. I can personally recommend KAP Audio, a multi-Grammy-winning editing and mixing facility. I have worked with Pete Pantelis at KAP Audio (facebook.com/

KAP-Audio-294627877235195/) for over twenty-five years and can attest to his excellence and professionalism. Pete has also contributed his expertise to many of the technical descriptions in this book.

The level of involvement you'll have with authors will vary from company to company. With smaller or indie publishing companies, you'll find some authors are eager to answer any questions you may have, and help with pronunciations of uncommon names or words. With major publishers, your questions about the book will more likely be discussed with your producer.

Check each publisher and casting site for their sign-up and submission procedures and their casting process. And remember, things are always changing; new companies form and established ones may change their focus and/or submission protocols, so it's important to do your research.

The following are a few online casting sites you'll want to explore:

ahabtalent.com, Penguin Random House's online talent site, is a platform to which you can upload audio clips and your profile.

acx.com (Audiobook Creative Exchange) is Audible's (owned by Amazon) platform on which you can be connected with producers and authors seeking actors to narrate their books. ACX also provides video tutorials for audiobook actors.

audiofilemagazine.com/referenceguide/, Audiofile Talent & Industry Guide, enables you to make your recording samples and resumé available to producers, directors and publishers.

thevoicerealm.com is an online casting site where producers submit scripts for which actors can then submit voice auditions. But all actors using the site (to date) must have access to "…broadcast recording facilities at no additional cost." Although it first appears that their site is for commercial voice overs, I checked with them, and, as of this writing, they confirm that they work with audiobooks as well.

Voices.com is a site where clients post jobs. The site notes that it uses its Voice Match algorithm to invite actors appropriate for that job. Actors invited then submit an audition and estimate of the cost to complete the job: voices.com/jobs/audiobooks

Backstage is a print and online trade publication geared to people in the performing arts. It often lists auditions for audiobook actors and these listings can be found online at backstage.com/casting/open-casting-calls/voice-over-auditions

findawayvoices.com (owned by Spotify) is a full audiobook production service. As part of their packages, they match authors with audiobook actors who are on the site.

upwork.com and **fiverr.com**, both websites working with freelancers, are places where you can find audiobook work.

VoiceCrafters is a website connecting companies and/or individuals with audiobook actors. The company notes that it provides actors who record in eighty languages: https://www.voicecrafters.com/

VO Planet is also a company featuring voiceover talent. They have a section dedicated to audiobook actors: voplanet.com/audiobook-narrators.

Voquent refers to itself as "the production platform made for storytellers." They feature actors speaking in, "Any language Any Accent." The section focusing on audiobook actors is titled: Hire Audiobook Narrators: voquent.com/narrators/

Other sites to investigate include: authorsrepublic.com, voice123.com, bunnystudio.com, and spokenrealms.com,

Compensation

How you'll be paid varies. Some companies pay per finished hour (PFH). This means you'll be paid an hourly rate for every hour of the finished audiobook's total running time (TRT). If it takes you ten hours to record a five-hour book, you'll be paid the PFH rate x 5. If it takes you fifteen hours to record that same audiobook, you'll still be paid the PFH rate x 5. Companies may differ in how many recording hours they expect you to need per each finished hour. If you're working in a studio the company has booked and is paying for, generally it's around two hours recording time per finished hour.

Other pay models differ. Some companies may pay a flat fee for the finished production. Another compensation option is a Royalty Share (RS). In this case you'll be paid nothing up front, but you'll share in the author's royalty income on the sales of the book.

Some audiobooks are recorded under the SAG-AFTRA union agreement covering audiobooks. As of this writing, over sixty-five publishers and producers are signatory to the SAG-AFTRA agreement. This means if you work with one of the signatories, you'll be working under the union agreement, which will stipulate minimum pay rates. These can differ depending on the publisher and type of production, so always be sure of the rate you'll be getting. If you're already a SAG-AFTRA member, great. If not, doing one audiobook under the SAG-AFTRA agreement will, currently, qualify you for membership. Always check with the union though, because regulations can change.

Industry Resources

SAG-AFTRA (Screen Actors Guild and American Federation of Television and Recording Artists) is the union that covers audiobook recordings. For information about membership, contracts, resources, etc., see: sagaftra.org

The Audio Publishers Association (APA). The APA is, in their words, "The Voice of the Audiobook Industry." They cover all aspects of the business, from publishing to technology to talent. They provide resources for libraries, publishers and artists, including information about conferences, get-togethers, festivals, seminars, etc. The Audie—a major award of audiobook industry—is awarded by the APA. Check their website for further information: audiopub.org

AudioFile Magazine is, as of this writing, considered the industry magazine. Published bi-monthly, it is available in print and online. The magazine is devoted to reviewing audiobooks and providing informative interviews with narrators, producers, and sometimes writers. Audiofile awards their Earphones Award to productions they consider outstanding. As previously noted, they publish the Audiofile Talent & Industry Guide, a comprehensive resource for the audiobook industry. Directors, producers and publishers can search this guide for talent by name, specific vocal skills and dialects. They can read uploaded resumés and find linked reviews of recent audiobook work. It's a great resource for audiobook actors: audiofilemagazine.com

Publishers Weekly magazine is another important source of information about the publishing industry, and their reviews of audiobooks are held in high regard. Available in both print and online: publishersweekly.com/pw/by-topic/industry-news/audio-books/index.html

The audiobook landscape is constantly changing. As the market continues to evolve and expand, new technologies, new companies and new opportunities will emerge.

What will always be at the center of the industry, however, is the creative, vital power of story telling and the audiobook actor.

I wish you joy in your career.

Appendix 1

Organizing Character Voices In An Audiobook Series

If you're working with a producer or director, they will likely oversee this for you.

If you are engineering as well as narrating the productions:

Prior to the session, create a Character List. Title it the name of the series, the name of the book, and list the characters in order of appearance. For example:

REKEISHA

ISAAC

CAROLE

JOHN

During the recording session, place a mark (a memory location) at each character's first bit of dialogue in the session timeline. Different recording systems may have different methods of marking, so always review the instructions for the system you are using.

Note the marker number next to each character on your list. It will look like this:

REKEISHA	1
ISAAC	2
CAROLE	3
JOHN	4

After the session create a Character Voice Audio file—a computer file—for the Character Voices you've marked, giving them the same marker numbers. Title the audio file with the name of the series and the book.

Alphabetize your Character List, keeping the original marker number next to the character's name. This will allow you to quickly locate each character and their marker. It will look like this example:

CAROLE	3
ISAAC	2
JOHN	4
REKEISHA	1

Create a Character List and Character Voice Audio File for the subsequent books in the series. Using this system, you'll more easily locate the Character Voice you need.

Appendix 2

The Possibles

1. Text: PHIL AND JIMMY G.

PHIL:

> Possible Character Key: Mid-50s, New Yorker, an old timer.
>
> Possible Character Voice: Gravelly, New York accent.
>
> Possible Objective: Establish rapport.
>
> Possible Actions: Advise, mentor.

JIMMY G.:

> Possible Character Key: 20s, from Brooklyn, thinks he's cool.
>
> Possible Character Voice: Higher pitched than Phil, Brooklyn accent.
>
> Possible Objective: To impress.
>
> Possible Actions: Tease, show off.

2. Text: THE EXISTENTIAL COWBOY

MIKE:

> Possible Character Key: 40s, fun loving, eager for excitement.
>
> Possible Character Voice: Baritone, urban, Standard American English accent.
>
> Possible Objective: Adventure.
>
> Possible Actions: Engage, get in the game.

SUZY:

> Possible Character Key: 30s, Los Angeles, flight attendant, sweet, accommodating.
>
> Possible Character Voice: High pitch, vocal fry.

Possible Objective: Mike's love.

Possible Actions: Be supportive, tease.

MONTE:

Possible Character Key: 50s, Floridian, cowboy, rugged, John Wayne type.

Possible Character Voice: Very low, powerful bass, western type Southern accent.

Possible Objective: Size Mike up.

Possible Actions: Be amenable, disarm.

TOM:

Possible Character Key: 50s, cowboy, wiry, good sense of humor.

Possible Character Voice: Higher pitched voice rises and falls as he speaks, some lip smacking, Oklahoma accent.

Possible Objective: Fun.

Possible Actions: Joke, tease.

3. Text: EMMA

EMMA:

Possible Character Key: 12½, New Jersey, White, very smart and talented, and very tween self-involved, everything she thinks, feels, experiences, is *uber* important.

Possible Character Voice: Very slight New Jersey accent, mid-range, talks fast, very dramatic.

Possible Objective: Emotional support.

Possible Actions: Confide, excite.

JENNY:

Possible Character Key: 12½, New Jersey, Asian-American, very gentle and sweet.

Possible Character Voice: Higher pitched, soft, no accent, sometimes whispery, has pauses in her speech.

Possible Objective: Make Emma feel good.

Possible Actions: Be supportive, be agreeable.

MARLA:

Possible Character Key: 12½, New Jersey, Black, loves science, analytic, wry.

Possible Character Voice: Lower pitched, warm, no accent, speaks very authoritatively.

Possible Objective: Reality-based conversation.

Possible Actions: Wake up her friend; inform or school her friend.

4. Text: EMMA AND JOSH

EMMA:

Possible Character Key: See #3.

Possible Character Voice: See #3.

Possible Objective: That Josh likes me.

Possible Actions: To joke, to cover.

JOSH:

Possible Character Key: 12, lives in Brooklyn, Standard American English accent, intelligent and sensitive.

Possible Character Voice: His voice changed early. It is mid-range. His speech is smooth, evenly paced, confident.

Possible Objective: That Emma likes me.

Possible Actions: Be cool, appreciate.

5. Text: JUSTIN AND SAM

JUSTIN:

Possible Character Key: 18, from West Texas, jock, loyal, caring, cockiness covers insecurity.

Possible Character Voice: West Texas accent, mid-range voice, assertive speech pattern.

Possible Objective: Keep his 'higher cool position' vis-à-vis his buddy.

Possible Actions: Tease, brag.

SAM:

Possible Character Key: 18, from West Texas, smart, coming into his own, excited about his future.

Possible Character Voice: West Texas accent, lower than Justin's, speaks with confidence.

Possible Objective: His friend's success.

Possible Actions: Encourage, support.

Glossary

A-B It: Compare two recorded tracks (such as when comparing track "A" with track "B"). You might compare voice tracks to ensure consistency in your sound after you've taken a long break, or when you resume a recording session the next day.

Baffling: Soundproofing material.

Button It: If your director asks you to put a "button" on it, or to "button it," you should give a definitive ending to the thought, the section, or the chapter.

Compression: Bringing the loud and soft parts of the audio signal closer together in level.

Control Room: The control room contains the equipment that records your reading. The engineer and director (also the producer and any visitors to the session) work in the control room.

De-Esser: Sometimes an audiobook actor's S's can sound whistly. A de-esser is either a piece of outboard gear or a computer plug-in that softens the hiss of the S's if you're unable to soften them yourself.

Director: The director's job is to guide the performance and ensure that the audiobook manuscript is read accurately and interpreted well. They will usually help the actor with pronunciations, foreign references, needed accents, etc. They'll also be on the alert to catch any errors in the text the actor is reading.

The Edit: The fully assembled read.

Editor: The editor assembles the selected takes, adjusts their volume levels, adds EQ when necessary, removes extraneous noises, and creates the final edit.

Engineer: The engineer records the performance, takes editing notes, and oversees sound quality.

EQ or Equalization: The process whereby certain frequencies in a track are boosted or diminished. For example, the highs might be boosted to give a voice a bit more presence, the lows to add some depth and warmth.

Executive Producer: This is the individual working at the publishing company who is responsible for overseeing the production of an audiobook.

Finished Hours: The length of the finished audiobook, also known as Total Run Time (TRT).

Home Studio: Your home studio is your recording booth. Audiobook actors create their studios in the best space available to them as long as it's quiet. As previously noted, a closet can become a studio.

Level: The volume at which something is recorded. If your reading has "shifting levels," this indicates that your voice varies in volume arbitrarily. This is not the same as acting dynamics, in which volume is intentionally varied for dramatic purposes. That is fine within certain parameters, but your level fluctuations can't be extreme.

Marking/Memory Location: During the recording session you "mark" the spot on the track, called a "memory location," where you first read a few sentences of a character's voice. Marking can help you maintain consistency of a character's voice, because if you forget how you voiced a character, you can go to its memory location to hear how you first voiced it. Note: Different recording programs can have different means of marking memory locations.

Master: This is the final audio file containing the mix of voice tracks, music, and sound effects. The master is sent on to the duplicator (the company creating multiple physical copies of the production if CDs are being manufactured) and/or to the company distributing the audiobooks online.

Mastering: This is the process wherein compression equalization, and noise reduction are employed to meet the standards of the industry and to make the recording sound as good as possible.

Microphone (Mic): There are a number of choices of microphones, and while several work well with most voices, it may be necessary to try various microphones to get the best sound for your voice. In almost every good professional studio there will be at least one of the Neumann family of mics, such as the U87, U89, or TLM 103. These are high-quality condenser mics, the first two offering a selection of pickup patterns, while the TLM 103 offers only a cardioid pick-up pattern.

A microphone's pickup pattern describes how it picks up sound directionally. A mic with a cardioid pickup pattern, for example, is unidirectional, meaning that it is most sensitive to sounds coming from one direction—directly in front of it—and much less sensitive to sounds coming from behind it. For an audiobook actor utilizing a cardioid mic, this means that too much head movement up or down or to the left or right can make the voice sound off-mic or in a different space. That's one of the reasons (another being noise) that audiobook actors learn to act with as little physical movement as possible.

Note: There are less expensive mics than the aforementioned Neumanns that are fine for use in home recording studios and are acceptable to audiobook publishing companies.

Mix: The combination of narration and music and sound effects. Some audiobooks are fully scored (they use a great deal of music and/or sound effects), some use theme music only at the beginning and end of the production, and others are voice only, with no music or sound effects.

Mouthy: Too much saliva can create little mouth noises as you speak. These noises are usually undetectable in conversation, but they are highly audible on a microphone. When this happens, you're said to be "mouthy."

Off-Mic: Your mouth is too far left, right, up, or down in relation to the mic.

Pickup: A pickup is just what it sounds like. You do a pickup when you've stopped recording, then "pick up" the reading again. You may do a pickup right where you stopped, or you may pickup the reading at an earlier spot. You may do a pickup for a particular line or for a word or words that you'll "punch in" later.

Playback: Playing back recorded material to listen to.

Plosives: A plosive is the sudden release of air into a mike which causes a popping sound. Consonants like P, B, F, W, are often the culprits. Th's can also cause this sound. While usually not noticeable in normal conversation, when spoken into a closely placed mic, plosives can sound like a mini explosions.

Pop Screen: The pop screen is a piece of mesh or screen placed in front of a microphone. It is used to soften plosives.

Post-Production: The work that is done after the recording session to create the finished production. This includes editing your best takes together, mixing, mastering, and adding music and/or sound effects.

  While the general terms used for post-production are described in this text, there are many sources you can access on and offline to learn about post-production's engineering, mixing, and mastering techniques.

Producer: The individual who is responsible for the overall production of the audiobook. This person may work at the publishing company or may be independent. Generally, the producer auditions and hires the audiobook actor, books the recording studio, and selects the engineer and/or editor. He or she also oversees the editor's work, providing notes and requesting corrections when required. The producer will book the post-production team and if needed, choose music and sound effects from music and sound effects libraries, or they may hire a composer and a sound designer. In many cases, the producer is also the director.

Publisher: The publisher is a company or individual responsible for acquiring, distributing and marketing the audiobook.

Punch In: A recording technique in which the engineer, when needing to rerecord (i.e., replace) just a portion of some previously recorded material that is perhaps marred by a noise or a mispronunciation of a word, or when returning to continue recording an unfinished track, starts the new recording from a specific place within the already recorded track, rather than rerecording the material again from the start.

QC (Quality Control): This is a review process to ensure that there are no text, factual, or production errors in an audiobook recording.

Raw Voice Tracks: The tracks you've recorded in their original form, prior to any editing.

Recording Booth: This is a soundproof room within a recording studio. Since audiobooks require many hours of recording per session, the recording booth should contain a comfortable, supportive chair. There will be a desk, a script stand, good lighting, and of course the microphone.

Recording Hours: The number of hours it takes to record the entire audiobook program, including all the takes.

Recording Studio: Professional recording studios vary in size, but all have two things in common: a control room and a recording booth.

Room Tone: The recorded ambient sound of the empty recording booth or other recording space.

SFX: Sound effects.

Take: A single performance of a particular portion of the script. It doesn't matter how large that amount is, a take goes on as long as the narrator keeps reading.

Talkback: Since the recording booth in a professional studio is soundproofed, when an engineer or anyone else in the control room needs to speak to you when you're in the booth, they'll speak into a "talkback mic," which is active only when a switch, the "talkback button," is pressed.

Too Hot: This means too loud. A spot in a recording that is "too hot" will sound distorted.

Track: A track is simply a recording of an individual audio element. It could be a voice track or a music track or a sound effects track.

About the Author

Taro Meyer is a Grammy-winning audiobook producer and director whose work has garnered Audie and Earphone awards. Her productions have been named to the lists for ALA Notable Recordings, the YALSA Top Ten, Publishers Weekly Annual Best of the Best, and Amazing Audiobooks for Young Adults.

A former actor and singer, Meyer starred on Broadway in *Zorba*, with Anthony Quinn, and in the miniseries *Memories of Midnight*, opposite Omar Sharif. She has also starred off Broadway and in daytime TV.

Meyer received Gold and Platinum Albums for her work with Trans-Siberian Orchestra's (TSO) management company and was co-producer of the multiple companies of TSO's arena show, *Christmas Eve and Other Stories*. She co-produced the TV Special, *The Ghosts of Christmas Eve* (PBS, FOX) and directed Ossie Davis in the narrated version of the album of the same name.

Meyer wrote and co-produced the children's album *Mighty Musical Fairy Tales*, starring international artist and Grammy winner Patti Austin. She is currently working on the development of a rock opera, *Tale of Two Cities*, with Krebs Communications Corporation.